Penguin Critical Studies

Coriolanus

Dr Stephen Coote was educated at Magdalene College, Cambridge, where he was an Exhibitioner, and at Birkbeck College, University of London, where he was the Senior Research Scholar. He is currently the Advisory Editor of the Penguin Passnotes series, to which he has contributed many studies of works of English literature. Dr Coote has also written on Chaucer and T. S. Eliot for the Penguin Critical Studies series. In addition, he has published a history of medieval English literature and biographies of Byron and William Morris.

Penguin Critical Studies
Advisory Editor: Bryan Loughrey

William Shakespeare

Coriolanus

Stephen Coote

Penguin Books

PENGUIN BOOKS

Published by the Penguin Group
Penguin Books Ltd, 27 Wrights Lane, London W8 5TZ, England
Penguin Books USA Inc., 375 Hudson Street, New York, New York 10014, USA
Penguin Books Australia Ltd, Ringwood, Victoria, Australia
Penguin Books Canada Ltd, 10 Alcorn Avenue, Toronto, Ontario, Canada M4V 3B2
Penguin Books (NZ) Ltd, 182–190 Wairau Road, Auckland 10, New Zealand

Penguin Books Ltd, Registered Offices: Harmondsworth, Middlesex, England

First published 1992
10 9 8 7 6 5 4 3 2 1

Printed in England by Clays Ltd, St Ives plc
Filmset in 9/11 pt Monophoto Times

Contents

Contents

Preface

Coriolanus is the last of Shakespeare's major tragedies and, it must be admitted, the least generally regarded. Among a body of work that measures the stature of European drama, the play is too often dismissed as 'the great toe of this assembly'. Reasons for such a view are not far to seek. The war between Rome and the Volsces has little of the conflict – geographical, ideological, emotional – that pits Antony against the splendid decadence of Cleopatra's Egypt. The domestic crisis in the play, although it triggers the catastrophe, lacks the sublime anguish and special music of *Othello*. If the work acknowledges something of the obsession with ingratitude seen in *King Lear*, there is little here of what Keats described as 'the strife betwixt damnation and impassioned clay' in that tragedy. Compared to the night-time horrors faced by Macbeth, the hero's 'lonely dragon' in his fen is almost a tame affair. Finally, compared to Hamlet, the hero of the Roman play can too easily be seen merely as a crass and militaristic boor.

Why then should we concern ourselves with a work that seems to provide so little of the familiar pleasure of Shakespearian drama, a tragedy that offers only a modicum of soul-searching poetry, few flights of fancy or grand soliloquies, and whose main characters appear largely unsympathetic? One reason – and it is the best possible – is that in the theatre such objections evaporate in the face of the dramatic tension, the concentrated, passionate yet remorselessly unillusioned power of Shakespeare's view of men and women as they struggle in their most human yet most unforgiving role as political animals. In this, *Coriolanus* is unsurpassed.

Coriolanus and the Humanist Tradition

No play can be written or received in a vacuum, and, while *Coriolanus* is for all time, it may be helpful to set it first in its particular cultural context. This requires us to sketch something of the development of humanism in Renaissance England. An understanding of humanism will in turn allow us to see why a hero of magnificent martial force but small education was so interesting to Shakespeare and his contemporaries, and why the play itself is so profoundly concerned with language and its political manipulation.

Though it has received a wide variety of interpretations since it was first coined in 1808, modern scholarly use of the term 'humanism' sees it principally as an educational and cultural movement concerned with the study of the Greek and Latin classics, a study which would in turn provide the education required to make a man (and, occasionally, a woman) fluent in the arts of rhetoric, or eloquent public persuasion.

Language and literature thus lay at the core of humanism, while humanist studies themselves were concerned with the moral and intellectual development of the whole being. In the words of John Milton, such an education 'fits a man to perform justly, skilfully and magnanimously all the offices, both public and private, of peace and war'. The student who, unlike the ill-educated hero of Shakespeare's play, had completed a full course of humanist studies was thus able to wield the powers of language and so take his full and effective place in the public and political world.

Both ancient poetry and ancient history were read in the pursuit of this educational purpose. Poetry, in the words of J. B. Trapp, was 'thought of as a guide to life, as philosophy hidden behind the veil of the letter, irresistible in the eloquence of its persuasion to the virtuous life'. History served an ancillary role, for it was considered to be the storehouse of moral example. It is in this context that we should appreciate Sir Thomas North's great endeavour in translating Plutarch's *Lives* out of a French version of the original and so providing Shakespeare with the source for his play. In addition, as any student tackling the first book of Livy's *History of Rome* would have learned:

The study of history is the best medicine for a sick mind; for in history you have a record of the infinite variety of human experience plainly set out for all to see;

and in that record you can find for yourself and your country both examples and warnings; fine things to take as models, base things, rotten through and through, to avoid.   (tr. A. de Sélincourt)

Both poetry and history were often subsumed by Renaissance scholars under the term rhetoric, or the conscious patterning and manipulation of language – the very skill, indeed, that was regarded as the crown of humanist studies. Peter Burke has written of this:

> The influence of rhetoric was apparent on what was put into the Renaissance history, as well as what was omitted. Histories usually contained set-pieces which gave the author a chance to show off his rhetorical skill. Their set-pieces included the 'character', or moral portrait of an outstanding individual; the description of action, particularly of a battle; and, most important of all, the speech.

The development of such rhetorical skills was the basic function of the grammar schools which had been founded (or refounded) in sixteenth-century England, such as the one at Stratford that Shakespeare himself attended. Here, in a tradition that stretched back to the ancient Greeks, boys would have learnt that speech is the foundation of human society and that, in the words of Isocrates, 'The power to speak well is taken as the surest index of a sound understanding, and discourse which is true and lawful and just is the outward image of a good and faithful soul.'

Though knowledge of Greek itself was comparatively restricted at this time, the ideas first given expression by Isocrates and his followers were developed and codified by the Latin rhetoricians Cicero and Quintilian. In the *Brutus*, his history of Roman oratory, Cicero declared that 'there is nothing that has so potent an effect upon human emotions as well-ordered and embellished speech'. We shall see that this is an idea of great significance to *Coriolanus*.

Both Cicero and, later, Quintilian in his *Institutio oratoria* (*Education of an Orator*) provided the rules for achieving this ideal of a use of language at once carefully ordered in its structure and richly embellished in its ornaments. While a full discussion of so large and important a subject is clearly not possible in the space available here, it will be interesting to examine at least some of the issues involved if only to establish the fact that Renaissance education was not a free exercise in imagination and self-expression, but a pursuit of a disciplined use of language in which intellectual control was the measure of a man's humanity. It was through these skills of rhetoric that contemporaries' own eloquence, logic and analytical abilities were judged, and such

3

rhetorical mastery remained the foundation of what some were to write and many more were to read or hear performed on the stage.

At the basis of all rhetorical training lay *imitatio* ('imitation'), the modelling of new compositions on the accepted masterpieces of past rhetorical excellence, whether these were in the 'judicial' (or legal) mode, exemplified the 'deliberative' rhetoric of persuasion, or developed the 'demonstrative' oratory of praise such as Shakespeare himself presents in Cominius' speech to the Senate in Act II of his play.

Cicero, Quintilian and contemporary manuals such as Thomas Wilson's *Arte of Rhetorique* also explained the skills or faculties required of the good rhetorician.

First came 'invention', the means of gathering together the material for a theme. The 'topics' – the tried and tested ways of approaching a subject – were one means of gathering material for this, while 'commonplaces' – pithily expressed maxims – were another. The character (*ethos*) of the speaker was also of importance in giving a speech moral weight, as were the raising of emotion (*pathos*) and the handling of logical argument. The use of examples (*exempla*) was often recommended, and Menenius' fable of the belly at the opening of *Coriolanus* is a particularly memorable employment of this device.

Having collected his material together, the orator had then to submit it to the discipline of 'arrangement'. This often consisted of dividing his argument into seven sections. Of these, the *exordium*, or opening, was designed to make hearers 'well disposed, attentive and receptive', as Cicero declared. Topics for the *exordium* often contained such devices as the 'modesty formula', the speaker's dignified suggestion of his own inability to perform the great task that lay before him – a device again used by Cominius at the start of his speech to the Senate.

This speech, as we shall see, continues with a vivid account of Coriolanus's deeds – what the rhetoricians, ever fond of naming their skills, called *descriptio* – enlivened in this case with *energia*, or vigorous description. Again, it was just such skills as these that sixteenth- and seventeenth-century schoolboys were required to cultivate, and by their teens many would have progressed to composing *chria* ('orations') arguing an ethical theme, or to constructing speeches appropriate to a hero or legendary character, a skill known as *prosopoeia*.

It will now be clear why a Renaissance play set in ancient Rome might be so profoundly concerned with language and its manipulation, but there are other aspects of a rhetorical training – of the skills familiar to every educated member of the original audience – that again have bearing on *Coriolanus*.

4

Memory, for example, was an essential rhetorical skill since ideally a speaker should talk without notes. While this is a faculty that is not of the greatest importance to *Coriolanus*, it is interesting to note that among the elaborate mnemonic devices with which a Renaissance speaker could picture the elements of his speech, the image of a theatre was often used.

Rather more important was delivery, or 'pronunciation'. Both voice control and the command of appropriate gesture were vital here, and if *decorum* were maintained in each, then, as Thomas Heywood explained in his *An Apology for Actors*, the orator revealed an advanced skill. 'A delivery and sweet action is the gloss and beauty of any discourse that belongs to a scholar.' In a passage that ends with words irresistibly reminiscent of Hamlet's advice to the players, Heywood continued:

To come to rhetoric, it not only emboldens a scholar to speak, but instructs him to speak well, and with judgement to observe his commas, colons and full points [full stops], his parentheses, his breathing spaces, and distinctions, to keep a decorum in his countenance, neither to frown when he should smile, nor to make unseemly and disguised faces in the delivery of his words, nor to stare with his eyes, draw awry his mouth, confound his voice in the hollow of his throat, or tear his words hastily betwixt his teeth, neither to buffet his desk like a madman, nor stand in his place like a lifeless image, demurely plodding, and without any smooth and formal motion. It instructs him to fit his phrases to his action, and his action to his phrase, and his pronunciation to them both.

It is with such ideas as these in mind that we should consider Coriolanus in the market-place hectoring the Citizens of Rome, losing his temper and behaving with the immoderate outrage of one who has not been schooled in the ways of oratory – an excuse which many of the other characters have frequently to make for him.

We might, by way of further contrast, compare these scenes from *Coriolanus* to the effect made by one of the greatest of all Jacobean orators, John Donne. Some lines by the obscure poet Jasper Mayne suggest how widely the skills of gesture were appreciated:

> Yet I have seen thee in the pulpit stand,
> Where one might take notes from thy look and hand
> And from thy speaking action bear away
> More sermon than some teachers use to say.
> Such was thy carriage, and thy gesture such,
> As could divide the heart, and conscience touch:
> Thy motion did confute, and one might see
> An error vanquish'd by delivery.

'Speaking action', gesture as argument: these are refinements of which we are almost wholly unaware today, yet to a Jacobean audience educated in a rhetorical tradition, people inspired by preachers uttering the most splendid of rhetorical sermons and entertained in a theatre where Shakespeare's princes could give advice on performance technique, the use of gesture was widely appreciated. Volumnia herself repeats the familiar rhetorical belief that 'Action is eloquence'; for her son, however, matters are usually rather different.

Yet it would be wrong to think that Coriolanus does not have an innate appreciation of the value of gesture. At the close of the climactic confrontation with his mother – at the moment when he has recovered his full humanity – the hero offers her his hand in a gesture of exemplary tenderness. It confirms that he will now make peace with his native city rather than destroy her in his wars. It is a gesture at once personal, political and, in the event, tragic.

Contemporary writers on these matters were well aware of the importance of hand gesture. In a rather curious work entitled *Chirologia; or the Naturall Language of the Hand*, John Bulwer declared:

How prevalent gestures accommodated to persuade, have ever been in the *Hand*; both ancient worthies, and also use and daily experience make good, it being a thing of greater moment than the vulgar think, or are able to judge of; which is not only confined to schools, theatres, and the mansions of the muses; but do appertain to churches, courts of Common Pleas, and the council table; where we daily see many admirable things done by those, who in the course of humanity and profitable studies, have been well instructed and informed in this faculty of the *Hand*.

Hand gestures can be of the greatest political potency, and in his moment of sublime pathos, taking his mother's hand, Coriolanus does indeed re-enter the human world – the world of rhetorical gesture. He does so, however, only to die.

What should now be evident from this brief and selective overview of humanism is the extreme importance of poetry, history and above all rhetoric to the education of that central figure in Renaissance thought, the universal man. This ideal was embodied for contemporaries in Castiglione's *The Book of the Courtier*, and Spenser's friend Gabriel Harvey wrote in his copy of that work:

Above all things it importeth a courtier to be graceful and lovely in countenance and behaviour; fine and discreet in discourse and entertainment; skilful and expert in letters and arms; active and gallant in every courtly exercise; nimble and speedy of body and mind; resolute, industrious and various in action; as profound and invincible in action as is possible; and withal ever generously bold, wittily pleasant and full of life in his sayings and doings.

This noble ideal is one of the great commonplaces of Renaissance thought and studies. It offers a rounded picture of aristocratic man as handsome, sociable, educated, physically resilient and maintaining an elegant balance between the public and the private. The soldier and the scholar are at one, language and action are in harmony.

The contrast to Shakespeare's hero – a figure magnificent on the battlefield but incapable of the easy use of controlled public language – is evident. The dangers of this untutored state were made clear by Plutarch himself in his biography of Coriolanus. They were also recognized by English writers of the Renaissance:

Ye know not what hurt ye do to learning that care not for words but for matter and so make a divorce between the tongue and the heart. For mark all ages, look upon the whole course of both the Greek and Latin tongue, and ye shall surely find that when apt and good words began to be neglected and properties of those two tongues to be confounded, then also began ill deeds to spring, strange manners to oppress good orders, new and fond opinions to strive . . . and . . . right judgement of all things to be perverted . . .

The corruption of the language is the corruption of the state, and Roger Ascham, the tutor of Elizabeth I, here calls the culture of ancient Rome to witness to the profound and potentially destructive relationship between politics and language that is also a central issue in *Coriolanus*.

The rhetorical culture of humanism forms an important background to a study of *Coriolanus*, but in the words of Inga-Stina Ewbank: 'Shakespeare learnt his language from men (and women) and books, from the Stratford grammar school and the London stage.' It is to this last we should now briefly turn.

The humanists' passion for the classics had led them inevitably to a study of Roman drama, in particular the closet plays conventionally attributed to the Roman philosopher Seneca. These works had been known during the Middle Ages, but the great flowering of English translation from the middle of the sixteenth century eventually resulted in a significant if fustian work, *Seneca, His Ten Tragedies*. The iambic fourteeners, heavy onomatopoeia and alliteration characteristic of these works was not suited to a fully theatrical realization, however, nor did Seneca's careful observation of the classical unities of time, place and action appeal to a taste for variety and spectacle. Though the Senecan conflict of private life and public duty – along with an interest in horrific events surmounted in mind at least by stoic heroes – was to prove widely influential, a new mastery of English verse and stage technique was required.

The early and didactic *Gorboduc* shows that vernacular writers were interested in dramatizing political themes, but it is with the tragedies of Marlowe and Kyd that the great period of tragic writing for the English stage begins. Marlowe's 'high-astounding' terms and heroes pitting new aspirations against older moral constraints offered fresh and revolutionary possibilities, while Kyd's *The Spanish Tragedy* (c. 1587) – a play that was to maintain its exceptional popularity throughout the period – provided spectacle, dialogue and rhetorical soliloquy in a manner that was equally influential. Seneca has here been transformed to help create the basis of a new English tradition, a tradition in which the stage is seen as a mirror of the world.

It was amid such vigorous experimentation with old forms and new approaches that Shakespeare himself learned his craft. His first tragedy, *Titus Andronicus*, takes a gruesome story from Roman history and, with somewhat self-conscious academicism, draws heavily on the classical past. Ovid was one important influence here, while Muriel Bradbrook (in *The Cambridge Companion to Shakespeare Studies*, ed. Wells) has written that '*Titus Andronicus* is a Senecal exercise; the horrors are all classical and quite unfelt, so that the violent tragedy is contradicted by the decorous imagery. The tone is cool and cultured in its effect.' Despite these failings, however, *Titus Andronicus* suggests a number of themes that were of great importance to Shakespeare's lifelong engagement with Rome and to his exploration of politics through the dramatization of Roman history.

In his excellent discussion of the play in 'Shakespeare and the traditions of tragedy', G. K. Hunter has shown that Shakespeare's presentation of his eponymous hero was designed to explore the moral chaos that ensues when a man holding rigidly to the moral system he believes supports his world is obliged to descend into the corrupt environment of daily events. In his absolute devotion to republican values, Titus is both horribly abused and hysterically vengeful: he loses his sons, his daughter is raped, and he himself is mutilated. Titus sacrifices another son who proves rebellious, while, as E. M. W. Tillyard (quoted in Bradbrook, see above) has shown, 'The culminating scene of Tamora eating her son's flesh in a pasty comes from Seneca's most popular play, the *Thyestes*.'

Coriolanus, it needs hardly be said, eschews such melodramatic effect, but its concern with the distortion of the personality through an absolute adherence to the supposed values of Rome is prefigured in *Titus Andronicus*, as is the challenge represented by the altogether more various values of other members of the body politic. As Hunter has written of *Titus Andronicus*:

Shakespeare is obviously anxious to create the most violent opposition possible between a morality based on unquestioning obedience and respect for the past, militaristic honour and strict hierarchy, and (set against that) a morality based on feelings, on the fulfilment of desires, with a fair tolerance for anarchy and discontinuity. The characters are ranged on either side of this divide, with no suggestion of possible compromise between them, so that all that can be achieved is a blood-bath followed by a new start for the few survivors – a not unusual Elizabethan model for tragedy.

In *Coriolanus* the perils of rigid integrity – the effects of this on both the individual and the society in which he lives – are juxtaposed to an unillusioned view of the equally distorting values held by other sections of Rome. These are respectively the vacillation of the mass of Citizens who are in turn so easily manipulated by Tribunes out to gain power through the distortion of language and opinion; the uncaring pragmatism by which most members of the aristocracy seek to maintain their power base; and finally, the machiavellian pursuit of prestige sought by Tullus Aufidius.

This greater range and, in particular, the place of language in the pursuit of power can be seen developing in Shakespeare's second Roman tragedy, *Julius Caesar*. The climactic moment in Act III scene ii of *Julius Caesar* when Antony mounts the pulpit in the market-place – a scene invented by Shakespeare rather than derived by him from Plutarch – focuses with the greatest clarity the play's concern with the diverse and warring elements in a Rome manipulated by language. At its centre is the death of the hero, a hero who is at once constant but tyrannical. Caesar himself makes these qualities in his character clear:

> I could be well moved, if I were as you;
> If I could pray to move, prayers would move me;
> But I am constant as the northern star,
> Of whose true-fixed and resting quality
> There is no fellow in the firmament.

> (III.i.58–62)

In so far as he is immune to the effects of language he is beyond the reach of sympathy. Such absolutism bears strong analogies to the Coriolanus of the early parts of the play, but, again like Coriolanus,

Critical Studies: Coriolanus

Caesar has no defence against the conspirator's sword. Both absolutists are cut down in the public gaze.

If political and personal absolutism rejects the emotional and persuasive power of language, Antony (like the Tribunes in *Coriolanus*) is magnificently able to manipulate rhetoric to his own advantage. Having genuinely lamented over Caesar's corpse, he turns to address a servant:

> Thou shalt not back till I have borne this corse
> Into the market-place; there I shall try,
> In my oration, how the people take
> The cruel issue of these bloody men;
> According to the which, thou shalt discourse
> To young Octavius of the state of things.
>
> (III.i.291–6)

'Friends, Romans, countrymen' is a speech magnificently designed to persuade for ruthless political purposes, a piece of demagoguery and rabble-rousing designed to foment chaos in Rome, turn the people against Brutus and the other conspirators, and so prepare for the terrifying proof that might is right at the start of Act IV where Antony divides up the world with Lepidus and the young Octavius Caesar.

Such manipulation of language and action will be developed with far greater unillusioned intricacy in *Coriolanus*, and, having suggested something of the cultural, theatrical and political context of the work, we should now turn to the play as a text for performance and observe the exceptional intellectual richness with which Shakespeare presented his analysis of the negotiations of political and personal values.

In doing this it is important to realize that productions at the Globe were played continuously. In other words, the structural divisions were not marked by the drawing of a curtain. Further, the usual division into five acts is almost certainly the work of the editors of the First Folio of Shakespeare's works (the only source we have for the play) and so reflects the conventions of a period later than that in which Shakespeare himself was working.

Following a suggestion in the admirable Penguin edition of the play, I see *Coriolanus* as falling into four basic units. With a gesture towards the play's profoundly humanist concern with rhetoric and the structuring of language, I have ventured to call these four units after the names made familiar to the Renaissance by J. C. Scaliger in his *Poetices* (1561) and subsequently given English definitions by Dryden in his *Essay on Dramatic Poesy* (1668).

The *protasis* introduces with remarkable dramatic skill the principal actors and conflicts: the Citizens of Rome, the patricians, the Tribunes, Tullus Aufidius, the Roman matrons and, above all, the hero. In the *epitasis* Shakespeare reveals his hero in his full and terrible military glory and so offers us the point of supreme achievement from which he will fall. The *catastasis* – the scenes which encompass Coriolanus's triumphant return to Rome and his subsequent ignoble rejection – are, when viewed in this way, surely to be seen as Shakespeare's supreme achievement in political drama. The ensuing *catastrophe* is one of his bitterest comments on political man.

These terms provide, I believe, a useful way of describing the structure of Shakespeare's play and allow us to see it once again as a work profoundly rooted in both theatrical convention and the traditions of Renaissance humanist scholarship. They are yet another means of seeing the play's overwhelming concern with the structuring of language and the manipulation of action.

Protasis

First, the Protasis, *or entrance, which gives light only to the characters of the persons and proceeds very little into any part of the action.*

Dryden: Of Dramatic Poesy

Act I scene i

The stage is an empty and silent space. Gradually, from all directions, groups of angry people begin to fill it. Their language is unclear, unscripted. Their gestures are threatening, but their purposes are not immediately obvious. Words and actions – the fundamentals of drama – are an incoherent, seething mass.

As more and more people swarm into view, their common energy begins to weld them into a whole, a mob, the 'company of mutinous Citizens' described by Shakespeare's stage direction. Gradually their collective being asserts itself. We are presented with what, to conservative members of the audience at least, was one of the most feared of phenomena: civil unrest and an image of the state divided against itself.

A leader emerges. The power of his language begins to bring some degree of control over action: 'Before we proceed any further, hear me speak.' The threatening action of the crowd has been brought to a standstill by words. Language has also given the First Citizen his role as leader. What before was incoherent and murmuring begins to take on shape and definition as the Citizens urge this nameless man to 'Speak, speak.'

We learn that famine has brought the Citizens to the point of desperation. They are prepared to take on the forces of authority rather than die of starvation. One figure of authority in particular, the man who for the moment we must call Caius Martius, is singled out as 'chief enemy to the people'. Whoever this man is, his naming at this point seems to establish the power of his personality and to suggest his antagonistic role in the class warfare that is wreaking havoc in the city. By being named, Caius Martius appears as an individual focusing the anger of the anonymous and collective mass. His death – the true tragic action of the drama – is seen as a panacea which will restore peace and

12

justice to the commonwealth. Excitement sweeps through the crowd as they resolve to kill him.

But a 'word' is raised in protest. The Second Citizen appears to be urging moderation. Language again seems to arrest action. The attempt is drowned, however, in the torrent of words that issues from the First Citizen. The first lengthy speech in the play is an enticement to violence. It is a form of rabble-rousing:

> Let us revenge this with our pikes ere we become rakes. For the gods know I speak this in hunger for bread, not in thirst for revenge.   (I.i.21–3)

Such an urging of civil disobedience may trouble us, but we also see that it is not without justification. The desperate hunger of the Citizens is all too evident, and it is clear that the aristocratic party – the patricians – have failed in their duty to provide any form of social cohesion. The rights and wrongs of the case are far from straightforward.

What is clearly evident, however, is that the body politic – what for Shakespeare was the natural order of society – has been unnaturally divided against itself. From this abuse of nature many varieties of chaos will spring. Instead of order and harmony, we have a world where dog eats dog – and the Citizens tell us that 'dog' is Caius Martius himself.

The Second Citizen again attempts to urge moderation, this time by an appeal to the patriotism of his fellows. He tries to kindle the feeling of reverence, of *pietas*, that every Roman should conventionally feel in the presence of the state. This he does by suggesting Caius Martius' greatness as a soldier. Such an appeal to military prowess suggests that the man himself is a national hero, a figure to be identified with the good of the state itself. Once again our view is confused: Caius Martius, it seems, is both pariah and hero.

But a cleavage between the state and its hero is also apparent. The actions of Caius Martius may well have brought glory to Rome. He cannot, however, be simply identified with the public good. There are private energies within him which seem to militate against this. We are told that he is 'proud' or 'partly proud' – the difficulty of defining the precise nature of this man is fundamental to the play – and that he is wholly under the sway of his mother.

Family and class loyalties again divide the state and differentiate the aristocrats from the plebeians, while Caius Martius' subservience to his mother is an odd and discordant note. It seems to suggest something boyish and immature in the martial hero. His valour or 'virtue' is freely

13

admitted, but it goes hand in hand with faults that are divisive and destructive. Once more the 'nature' of the hero is presented as a complex matter. But the discussion of Caius Martius' 'nature' seems to get trapped in the very language by which it must be analysed. We feel that he eludes an easy understanding, as well as sensing that violent action has itself become trapped in words.

'Shouts within' resolve the dilemma. The language of violence in another part of the city rekindles the fury of the mob. Reasoned words and analysis are immediately beside the point. 'Why stay we prating here?' The commanding language of the First Citizen urges the Citizens to storm the Capitol, the seat of government. Words are about to give place to anarchy.

Once again, however, violent action is postponed. The entrance of the aristocratic Menenius Agrippa has a calming effect. His placatory role is recognized, along with the fact that he seems 'honest enough'. His string of questions apparently reintroduces some degree of intellectual control. Again the First Citizen is asked to speak. Perhaps language will once more moderate the fury of the mob.

The anger of the First Citizen is indeed slightly less acrimonious than before. None the less, his speech suggests how words of advice and caution are now at breaking point and that, with their collapse, the energies they contain will spill over into violence.

It is the duty of the aristocratic politician to try and prevent this, and we have seen that the recognized means of doing so is language – a language patterned into the eloquent and persuasive forms of rhetoric. Virgil, the greatest poet of ancient Rome and a figure familiar to every scholar, gave a vivid and celebrated account of the political use of rhetoric in the opening book of the *Aeneid*, his epic poem on the history and customs of Rome. The passage contains interesting analogies to the first scene of *Coriolanus*.

Virgil tells how the founding fathers of the Roman empire have been caught in a terrible storm at sea which only the might of Neptune can control. Eventually the seas quieten down and Aeneas and his crew are saved:

It had been like a sudden riot in some great assembly, when, as they will, the meaner folk forget themselves and grow violent, so that firebrands and stones are soon flying, for savage passion quickly finds weapons. But then they may chance to see some man whose character and record command their respect. If so, they will wait in silence, listening keenly. He will speak to them, calming their passions and guiding their energies. So, now, all the uproar of the ocean subsided.

(tr. W. F. Jackson-Knight)

Virgil sees storms and mobs as threats to the Roman state, and he compares the power of the orator who can calm a crowd to the power of a god who can calm the seas. In addition, he goes to some lengths to point out the personal qualities that make up the true orator. He is nobly born, even-tempered, a man of established character, education and record. He is a figure of respect, and his language will guide the emotions back to their proper place under the control of reason. Virgil's speaker is an embodiment of *romanitas*, the values of ancient Rome.

And it is an image of the might and moral worth of ancient Rome that Menenius now attempts to put forward. His speech appears as a model of all the Roman state held dear. Menenius himself thus takes on the role of the spokesman or orator of Roman values.

First he urges the 'charitable care' of the patricians (a care we may already be questioning even as he mentions it) and then suggests that to resist a famine sent by fate is as futile as to try and resist the Roman state itself, a political entity which, as Virgil had suggested, was the special creation of Fate herself. Menenius' subsequent image of Rome as a war machine marching on irresistibly to universal triumph is a vital element in our understanding of Shakespeare's presentation of Rome in the play. All little men are swept up in its great, impersonal purposes:

> For your wants,
> Your suffering in this dearth, you may as well
> Strike at the heaven with your staves as lift them
> Against the Roman state, whose course will on
> The way it takes, cracking ten thousand curbs
> Of more strong link asunder than can ever
> Appear in your impediment.

> (I.i.64–70)

The response of the First Citizen to this idealized, though far from ideal, image of the state is to assert the facts as he knows them: a life of exploitation, poverty and hunger. The vivid language of prose contempt is juxtaposed to the high (and, as we shall see, ultimately spurious) rhetoric of Menenius' speech. The role of the great orator has failed to work the desired effect, and the angry honesty of the First Citizen begins to rouse our suspicions. How sincere have Menenius' words been? We begin to wonder if rhetoric really is a form of deceit. After all, how genuine is the noble role Menenius has adopted? Is there perhaps a divide between his language and real intention? What are his words really worth?

Menenius' response to this dangerous situation is to tell a parable, a

15

low form of rhetoric that classical orators regarded as suitable for children and common people of small education. Menenius' manipulative character thus becomes more evident, and our sympathies perhaps join with the suspicions of the First Citizen: 'you must not think to fob off our disgrace with a tale.'

This is, none the less, what Menenius proceeds to do, and the result is a grotesque and cynical episode. High rhetoric having failed to persuade the Citizens of the worth of the aristocracy, the manipulative patrician now proceeds to condescend and caper before them, lacing his antics with abuse. He takes the venerable image of the state as a body (what we still sometimes call 'the body politic') and proceeds to use it to his own advantage.

The underlying idea here is that just as the human body has parts and functions of varying degrees of nobility, so the body of the state is made up of various classes ranged in hierarchies of worth. The stomach (or aristocracy) takes in all the body's necessary supplies of food and, in theory, distributes these fairly to the various other members. In Menenius' fable, however, these lesser but hard-working organs have grown resentful, and he has to contrive the belly's answer.

Menenius begins by making the belly smile. We should perhaps think at this point of the cynical patrician creasing the folds of his ample stomach to amuse the plebeians, men whose own stomachs are all but empty. We have seen that the orator's art of gesture was regarded as an extremely important aspect of his skills, and much attention was given to perfecting its nobility. Menenius' gesture here, however, is grotesque – a comic and condescending image of his well-fed patrician cynicism. Rhetoric has slipped to mere exploitative vulgarity, and the speech of the First Citizen (rising for the first time from the prose of the mob to the dignity of poetry) suggests something of his own inherent dignity. The patrician party is demeaning itself.

Menenius' quick-wittedness none the less allows him to get the better of the First Citizen, even while we begin to despise him. He continues with his parable. Though the stomach receives all the food at first, he says, it is its duty to distribute it fairly to the other members of the body. This Menenius claims (in spite of all the evidence to the contrary) the stomach, or aristocracy, actually does. 'I can make my audit up.' And what does the stomach get in return for all this effort? Merely the 'bran'.

Menenius then proceeds to draw a parallel between the physical body and the body politic. Just as the hard-working stomach seems to be the source of all the body's welfare and to receive very little credit for this, so the patricians – he says – are the source of all the benefits the common people of Rome receive.

This is no answer to give starving people, and Menenius, aware perhaps of its futility and the Citizens' growing impatience, resorts to sarcasm. Developing the parallel between the human body and the body politic, the First Citizen (a man who has now risen considerably in our estimation) is derided by Menenius for being 'the great toe' of the company. Asked to explain himself, Menenius resorts to mere abuse. The 'great toe', he says, is that on which the wretched body politic springs forward to ask for favours and on which it quickly runs away in times of peril. The plebeians, in other words, are merely self-seeking cowards.

It is probable that at this stage in a production, the barely articulate fury with which the Citizens opened the play should rise to a crescendo. Menenius has just mentioned their cowardice in war and now, as their fury rises, his images of fighting become images of civil strife, of the Roman state disastrously divided against itself. So much for the ideal of the honest rhetorician bringing about public peace. Menenius' manipulative cynicism has failed. 'Rome and her rats are at the point of battle.' Language has all but lost its power to contain the violence that may soon issue in anarchy. It is a moment of terrible political peril.

Enter Caius Martius. The entry of the hero is both profoundly dramatic and profoundly ironic. Rome is at the very point of civil war. Her great hero (and the man who will soon work to contrive her almost certain destruction) subdues the forces threatening to pull her apart. His language is the measure of the man:

> What's the matter, you dissentient rogues,
> That rubbing the poor itch of your opinion
> Make yourselves scabs?
>
> (I.i.162–4)

The imagery is violent, repulsive and suggestive of self-destruction. As such, it is indicative both of the theme of the play and the nature of the hero. There is an uncouth, all-mastering aggression here – the savagery of the extreme political right – which may cow men to a temporary civil obedience but which is both destructive and ultimately self-destructive. Its unthinking, spontaneous fury is the very opposite of the political and social notions enshrined in the ideals of rhetoric. This is language as a cudgel.

We might turn to Shakespeare's source material at this point. A major part of Plutarch's concern was to draw general moral lessons from the lives of the particular heroes he portrayed. His fascination with the figure of Coriolanus lay in his being a man of great valour and little education in a society where 'valiantness was honoured ... above all other virtues'. Plutarch describes the resulting dilemma thus:

This man is ... a good proof to confirm some men's opinions, that a rare and excellent wit untaught doth bring forth many good and evil things together, like a fat soil bringeth forth herbs and weeds that lieth unmanured. For this Martius' natural wit and great heart did marvellously stir up his courage to do and attempt notable acts. But on the other side, for lack of education, he was so choleric and impatient, that he would yield to no living creature: which made him churlish, uncivil, and altogether unfit for any man's conversation.

This is the crux of the hero's tragic dilemma. On the one hand we have a man whose courage is an enormous national asset and an epitome of all that his society holds dear. On the other hand, a lack of education – a fundamental barbarity – makes it impossible for him to be contained within the very society that validates his worth.

Plutarch develops this idea and then goes on to point his moral:

... his behaviour was so unpleasant to them by reason of a certain insolent and stern manner he had, which because it was too lordly, was disliked. And, to say truly, the greatest benefit that learning bringeth unto men is this: that it teacheth men that be rude and rough by nature, by compass and rule of reason, to be civil and courteous, and to like better the mean state than the higher.

The violence of aristocratic pride and martial worth, the scorn of an uneducated hero of the right, are clear in the torrent of abuse Caius Martius directs to the Citizens of Rome. These, he says, are people on whom 'good words' would be squandered. The only appropriate language is disdain, and the imagery with which he heightens his contempt is interesting. The Citizens are base animals. They have no ability whatsoever to judge the true worth of a great man. They are wholly untrustworthy and vacillating.

All of these are ideas the play will develop in some depth, and not the least irony is that many of Martius' opprobrious epithets will eventually be applicable to himself. We will see that praise and flattery, the use of 'good words', is something to which he will be peculiarly sensitive. As his role in the play develops, we will see him as man, as superman and also as an animal, a solitary beast existing in lonely exile from his community. That exile will stem in large part from the problems of judging the worth of the great man – something Martius claims the Citizens are singularly incapable of doing and which, as the text has already suggested, is a particularly difficult process anyway. But the greatest irony lies in his accusing the Citizens of being untrustworthy and vacillating in their judgements. This is the man, we may care to remember, who will turn against his own city and try to work its destruction.

None the less, in a play where the process of moral judgement is of particular complexity – a play in which Shakespeare works towards an ever more objective and unillusioned view of political man – we must also recognize that there is much truth in what Martius has to say at this point. The Citizens will indeed prove themselves to be cowardly and vacillating. They will indeed be incapable of judging the worth of a great man. Flattery is not an appropriate language for an honest politician to greet them with.

Nor are the Citizens adequately informed about the proceedings of an essentially aristocratic government. Martius' description of them sitting by their firesides and presuming to know what is done in the Capitol has, we may feel, a large element of truth about it. None the less, this involvement of the ordinary people in the political process is a point of great importance, and one which Shakespeare handles with a sure mastery of dramatic surprise. On the one hand Martius' continued abuse – the absurdly destructive violence which causes him to say that he would slaughter such people – reinforces our negative view of him as a political figure. On the other hand, for many members of a Jacobean audience at least, the idea that the Citizens should have their elected representatives in the Capitol raised the equally frightening prospect of full democracy.

To see *Coriolanus* in its proper historical perspective we have to imagine a situation where a powerful Crown was often strongly opposed to Parliament, and that Parliament itself was seen as the mouthpiece of the propertied classes only. In such a world full democracy was for most anathema, an invitation to certain chaos. *Coriolanus* will illustrate a similar thesis. This does not, as we shall see, deprive it of very real and continuing political interest. Shakespeare's understanding of how small elected élites may manipulate the mass for personal advantage – the sheer self-seeking cynicism of small-time politicians – is chillingly accurate and raises lasting objections to any too rosy view of the political process.

Martius himself, of course, sees the election of the Tribunes as a political disaster, and events will in large part justify this view. The Tribunes will indeed be spurs to 'insurrection's arguing'. The embattled language of political debate will indeed ferment civil strife. Words once again are seen as extremely powerful and dangerous, the stimulants of a violence they cannot always contain.

Throughout this first scene there has been a constant interplay between language and violence, words and action. Now, it appears, that pent up violence can be usefully released in the service of the state. A messenger enters hastily to tell us that the Volsces, the enemies of Rome, are in arms. Martius is delighted. War will direct internal conflict outwards: 'we shall ha' means to vent/Our musty superfluity.' The imagery may make us recall Menenius' fable of the body. Now, the body politic will be armed.

With the arrival of the Senators, we hear something of great interest about the Volsces from Martius:

> They have a leader,
> Tullus Aufidius, that will put you to't.
> I sin in envying his nobility,
> And were I anything but what I am,
> I would wish me only he.
>
> (I.i.226–30)

It is apparent that Martius sees the rivalry between the Romans and the Volsces largely in personal terms; the mere mention of the name of Tullus Aufidius forces him to assert his own sense of self. Clearly, he sees Tullus Aufidius as a rival in 'nobility'. At once the whole aristocratic ethos of honour is brought vividly before us. And crucially, with honour, comes shame. To envy someone so noble as Tullus Aufidius is a 'sin'. The language suggests the mystic qualities with which aristocracy is imbrued in Martius' mind, and it is essential to appreciate the quasi-religious awe with which he regards these foundations of his personal faith. As a man's faith is, so is his life, and a faith in 'nobility' – in the chivalrous life of arms and glorious reputation – is crucial to an understanding of the entire play.

However, if the mere mention of the name of Tullus Aufidius rouses Martius' sense of self, it also profoundly questions it. Other than himself, Martius cannot imagine another man he would rather be than Aufidius. In other words, his sense of personal identity is so closely bound up with his perceptions of what Tullus Aufidius represents that Martius feels personally threatened by him. This alerts us to the danger of the Roman hero's perception of political conflict in purely personal terms while giving a first and very subtle indication of the identity of the hero with his enemy. This, after all, is the man who will defect to the rival he both hates and loves and without whom his existence cannot be extended to the full. Given the opportunity, Martius would make 'only my wars with him'.

For the moment, the aristocratic company of Senators interprets this as the natural hyperbole of a noble warrior. They rejoice in the apparent implication of Martius' words – that he is desperately keen to engage with his country's enemies. The deeper and more ambiguous implications of egocentric honour and confused identity pass them by. It is in these, however, that the tragedy will partly lie.

We are told that Martius is to fight under the leadership of the older Cominius, and we see the aristocrats, after a brief exchange of the courtesies so characteristic of their class, exiting to the Capitol. To heighten the sense of the social divisions in Rome, Shakespeare juxtaposes the polite exchanges of these men to Martius' final flourish of abuse at the Citizens.

A lesser dramatist might have been content to end the scene here. We have seen the political situation in Rome and glimpsed the major characters involved, and we have begun to develop some complex responses to the issues and personalities engaged in the crisis. But Shakespeare does not leave us with our own responses. For the first time we meet the Tribunes of the people.

At first they voice what seem to be natural reactions to Martius' pride, but beneath the surface of these we can perhaps detect elements of jealousy and rivalry which express themselves through the tone of apparent exaggeration. Their real hatred of the complex national hero emerges through a brilliantly contrived use of irony.

Martius had expressed the hope that the war with the Volsces would be a means of subduing the Citizens; a conflict with the enemy without would thus be a means of subduing what he sees as the enemy within. The Tribunes, in what now becomes their own evident desire for power, see the war as a means of destroying Martius, their enemy within the state. The war that might have united the city becomes the means of showing its range of divisions: aristocrats against Citizens, Citizens against aristocrats and a third group – the Tribunes, the cynical manipulators of the people – seeking their own advantage amid the rival factions.

Shakespeare suggests the cynical nature of the Tribunes with consummate dramatic economy. Rather than have them discuss the Citizens whom they claim to represent, they discuss Martius. The hero thus remains the focus of debate, while the Tribunes' attempts to define his behaviour actually reflect on the way they themselves think about power.

21

Sicinius is surprised that Martius can 'brook' to be commanded by another man. Brutus explains (with a refinement of cynicism wholly beyond Martius' abilities) that this is in fact a wise move since anything that goes wrong will be blamed on Cominius while all that goes well will rebound to Martius' honour. These are the words of men who have inveigled themselves into power on the basis of very little personal integrity and who assume that all men operate thus; Martius, we feel sure, is innocent of such manipulation. Such dialogue tells us little about the hero's true nature, a great deal about how words may misinterpret deeds and, above all, a great deal more about the nature of the Tribunes themselves.

All of this is a supreme dramatic achievement. In fewer than 300 lines, Shakespeare has unfolded the complexities of a political situation, vividly suggesting class warfare, the highly ambiguous nature of his hero, and the range of themes he will develop throughout the play. The rest of the *protasis* will be given over to his equally accomplished presentation of the other leading figures in the drama.

Act I scene ii

The purpose of the second scene is to introduce Tullus Aufidius. This presents a particular dramatic problem, since it was essential for Shakespeare to draw a contrast between two men whose similarities he had been much preoccupied in establishing in the first scene. Shakespeare's solution is masterly. He manages to make Tullus Aufidius a distinct individual while, at the same time, elaborating some of the play's central themes.

We have seen that Martius' response to the mention of Tullus Aufidius' name was at once to assert his own sense of self and to suggest how this is intimately involved with the existence of his rival. Such an ambiguous relationship between Tullus Aufidius and Martius, and thus between the Volsces and the Romans – this sense of identity in rivalry – is again clear from the opening lines of the second scene:

> So, your opinion is, Aufidius,
> That they of Rome are entered in our counsels
> And know how we proceed.
>
> (I.ii.1–3)

We are introduced to the world of spies and double agents in a play whose hero will desert his own people to form an alliance with the enemy. The duplicitous and ambiguous relationship between the two enemies is established. So, too, is Tullus Aufidius' personality. The emotional violence we associate with Caius Martius is replaced by what appears to be a cool-headed pragmatism. Aufidius calmly produces what we know to be the accurate reports of his own intelligence network, but beneath the surface of high honour is a world of duplicity and advantage seeking – a world which characterizes Shakespeare's entire view of politics in the play.

Our sense of Aufidius' practical cunning is enhanced by his subsequent speech, but we are also made aware of the very real military ability of the Romans. They have used the information gathered by their intelligence agencies to get their army into the field far earlier than Aufidius expected and so have frustrated his plan to take in a number of minor towns before sacking Rome.

There is an interesting contrast to be drawn between Martius being ordered to the field in the first scene and Aufidius being given his commission here. Where Martius thrilled with a complex and highly emotional excitement, seeing the war as a duel of personal honour and a means of allaying what he views as the political troubles at home, Aufidius is altogether more measured in his response. His principal interest appears, at least, to be tactics. His first words are concerned with military preparations. Only after mentioning these does he refer to Martius and then, while the personal involvement with his great rival is clear, it is altogether a more measured excitement than that expressed by Martius.

The end of the scene is correspondingly brief and efficient. It remains to be seen, however, how far Aufidius' presentation of himself as a polite, level-headed and shrewd young military man is a role covering deeper and more problematic levels of character.

Act I scene iii

The two opening scenes of the play have presented us with masculine worlds, worlds at once public and political. Shakespeare now offers us the feminine and domestic sphere: the world of the Roman matrons.

This last phrase is of importance in determining our attitude to the scene and the characters it presents. The ideal of the Roman matron – a figure wholly feminine yet endowed with forms of physical courage and moral fortitude more conventionally associated with men – was one that greatly interested the Renaissance. As we might expect, the figure derives from classical literature and is to be found in the works of historians such as Livy and poets such as Virgil. Shakespeare had presented the type before in his earlier Roman plays, for example Portia in *Julius Caesar*. Volumnia is, however, his most comprehensive working of the image and an essential part of the *romanitas* – the ethos of ancient Roman civilization – that he is concerned to analyse in *Coriolanus*. She is a figure who will rise to awesome stature.

The scenes that we have been presented with so far have been constructed out of a very wide range of language, a variety of speech which gives the play its dramatic and thematic richness. This scene almost certainly opens in silence. The hero's wife and mother enter and then: 'They set them down on two low stools and sew.' The atmosphere is domestic, introverted and slightly sad.

Volumnia breaks the silence and her speech at once begins to unfold the *romanitas* embodied in the figure of the Roman matron. Making war is presented as superior to making love, the violent and the public to the intimate and private. At the basis of all right action lies 'honour', that quintessentially aristocratic virtue worshipped by Caius Martius who has been bred to it by his mother:

To a cruel war I sent him, from whence he returned his brows bound with oak. I tell thee, daughter, I sprang not more in joy at first hearing he was a man-child than now in first seeing he had proved himself a man.   (I.iii.13–17)

Volumnia has nursed her son to be the image of a perfect Roman. With his brows bound with oak, he is as representative of his culture as a profile on a coin or a figure on a triumphal arch. He is *romanitas* personified.

Yet we are almost certainly bound to question the implications of Volumnia's speech. What is the nature of this culture that sends boys to 'cruel' wars? While Western countries in the twentieth century are, on the whole, rather more circumspect in their treatment of youngsters than this, we might ask how Shakespeare's audience would have reacted to the use of this adjective by the hero's mother.

Again, the phrase 'man-child' conventionally meant a baby boy, yet the context here reveals a telling ambiguity. There is a flickering suggestion – a suggestion which the unfolding of the play will develop to tragic proportions – that Martius is both a man and a child, a child and a man. Of all the insults hurled at him by his enemies, 'boy' is the one that hurts him most. We know already that he has a devotion to his mother which, while not unnatural, is none the less sufficiently pronounced to be a feature of his behaviour worthy of comment.

We are thus shown a world where childhood seems to have no status beyond being a reflection of the adult world, a bias which the seventeenth century was perhaps more willing to accept than we and which yet appears strained when voiced by mothers. Indeed, these mothers seem to lack something of the tender and nourishing qualities that are conventionally associated with women. Above all there remains the irony that these women, so conspicuously given to rearing martial men, actually produce in Caius Martius a soldier who is felt at once to be both a superman and a boy – a 'man-child'.

Such are some of the dubious areas that underlie the explicit values of Shakespeare's Roman matrons. Yet this highly complex scene is related to other of the play's themes with great delicacy. The announcement of the arrival of Valeria prompts the exploration of these and is a further example of the richness and economy of Shakespeare's dramatic method.

In the absence of her husband, Virgilia wishes to preserve her privacy and silence. Later we learn that she has made a resolve: 'I'll not over the threshold till my lord return from the wars.' Such modesty was considered entirely proper, a true decorum. In a play that is so greatly concerned with language, however, this issue of keeping one's word and so preserving integrity is of great interest. Juxtaposed to Volumnia's extreme assertion of public male values (values which make Hector's bloody forehead a more beautiful image than the breasts of Hecuba) is Virgilia's quiet, withdrawn fixity of purpose.

This silence and resolve are also contrasted to Valeria's dialogue, speeches which add yet another level of linguistic richness to this scene and to the play as a whole. So far the scene has shown us Volumnia's somewhat masculine force and contrasted it to Virgilia's reticence. Two images of the Roman matron are thus created through speech. Now, with Valeria, we are offered that fluttering, allusive and literary discreetly enthusiastic tone that marks the well-bred society lady. The presentation of Roman matronhood is thus enriched with a third element.

Children and social visits – what we might perhaps expect to be the subject of noblewomen's talk – are discussed. However, even Caius Martius' son's playing with the butterfly is seen in 'one on's father's moods' (an early image of a future war machine), thus keeping the more questionable elements of *romanitas* firmly in our minds.

What is perhaps most interesting about the scene is the two other women's varied and persistent attempts to make Virgilia break her word and go visiting with them. Throughout the play, language is used as a means of persuasion, often for ends that are far from honest or straightforward. Here the intention is relatively harmless, but the

25

persuasion does not work. Virgilia remains constant, true to her word. In this she suggests a fundamental integrity, a fixed moral resolve that lies at the very centre of the ideal of the Roman matron. In this small but important way she makes an all but silent comment on the play's preoccupation with integrity of purpose, and language as a means of persuasion and manipulation.

At the close, having told us that Caius Martius and his soldiers have 'set down' before the enemy city, Valeria leaves. All the main characters have now been introduced to us, the *protasis* is at an end, and Valeria's news prepares us for the next section.

Epitasis

Secondly, the Epitasis, *or working up of the plot where the play grows warmer – the design or action of it is drawing on and you see something promising that it will come to pass.*

Dryden: Of Dramatic Poesy

Act I scene iv

Shakespeare is now to show us his hero in his full and awesome magnificence. After exposition comes action. Relatively brief though it is, the *epitasis* is an exceptionally vigorous passage, and in studying the text it is more than ever necessary to use both the visual and aural imaginations.

The rapid exchange between Caius Martius and Titus Lartius at the opening suggests the speed and excitement of what is to ensue. This is the conversation of men thrilled by the prospect of imminent action. The courteous banter about the horse also suggests the aristocratic world from which these figures come. In such ways the major themes of the play are kept subtly in mind.

Even the one line of the Messenger's speech helps in this. Asked whether the two armies have engaged, he replies: 'They lie in view, but have not spoke as yet.' The use of the second verb is particularly interesting. We have seen that *Coriolanus* is a work profoundly concerned with the relationship between language and action; here the two are identified. Warfare is seen as speech. Language and deeds are one. This is the first suggestion of a theme that will play an increasingly important role as the tragedy develops.

The repeated trumpet sounds heighten the martial mood, and, as the blood of the hero races ever faster, he offers a short prayer to the god of war: 'Now Mars, I prithee, make us quick in work.' That a soldier should make such a prayer is entirely appropriate, but we may also find it suggestive that Caius Martius should call on the god from which his second name (the name of his family) derives. Later in the play, as the attempts to define the nature of the hero become ever more elaborate, he will be explicitly compared to the god of war. That Caius Martius is in some respects Mars himself – literally a 'son of Mars' – enhances his nature as a superman. Names, those most intimate of words, are of great thematic importance in the play, and at the close of the *epitasis* Caius Martius himself will acquire a new one; he will become 'Coriolanus'.

Meanwhile, the battle itself must be fought. The ritual exchange of verbal hostilities between Martius and the First Senator of the Volsces prepares us for this. Language is now an expression of violent intention and, once again, the sound effects – first a far-off drum and then a distant alarm – increase the tension. It is Martius' exclamation, 'O, they are at it!' that most vividly conveys his own excitement, his exultation in the prospect of blood and death. This is indeed the man who can be completely identified with warfare. We may well be appalled (as in part we are surely meant to be), yet it is important to go beyond this and realize the exceptional emotional force that surrounds a figure who is the embodiment of one of mankind's most fundamental impulses.

This sense of horrified awe is essential to our understanding of Shakespeare's purpose and, as we might expect, Martius' complete identification with his role has a profound effect on his language. He now speaks as a great general, a stern and inspiring leader whose words are an enticement to heroism:

> Now put your shields before your hearts, and fight
> With hearts more proof than shields. Advance, brave Titus.
> They do disdain us much beyond our thoughts,
> Which makes me sweat with wrath. Come on, my fellows.
> He that retires, I'll take him for a Volsce,
> And he shall feel mine edge.
>
> (I.iv.24–9)

This is a very different language to that Martius used in the first scene of the play. There, language was a form of violence directed at the Citizens, and its speaker took a perverse pleasure in its bludgeoning power. Though the note of contempt is still there, particularly in the last two lines, such hostility now serves a very different purpose: it is used to inspire the mass of men grouped before the speaker. And those men are no longer a 'common cry of curs' but 'my fellows'. Only when exhilarated by his role as a soldier in the field of action does Caius Martius feel able to use the language that binds him to his community. In this we see both his excellence as a soldier and his disastrous limitations as a man who has no civil existence beyond the killing fields.

For the moment, though, language has done all it can do. It has been used as an enticement to action, and now that action is presented to us:

'Alarum. The Romans are beat back to their trenches.' In places such as this it is above all necessary to imagine the play on the stage and to think of drama in its true role as the representation of action. The varied languages of the play have been strained to the limit throughout by the forces of violence. Now those forces break out – and lead to temporary defeat for the Romans.

Enter Martius, cursing. His own forces have betrayed the hero in the one area where his magnificence can be displayed. The language of inspiration and encouragement used before the engagement is replaced by its opposite. Violence and abuse are poured on the citizen army. This utter contempt of the martial aristocrat for the people returns Martius to his familiar role:

> All the contagion of the south light on you,
> You shames of Rome! You herd of – Boils and plagues
> Plaster you o'er, that you may be abhorred
> Farther than seen, and one infect another
> Against the wind a mile! You souls of geese
> That bear the shapes of men, how have you run
> From slaves that apes would beat!
>
> (I.iv.30–36)

His erstwhile 'fellows' are now less than men, and, in a train of imagery that is of great importance to the play, what is less than man is an animal. Such beings are the 'shames of Rome'. They have no place in the community.

Berated thus, the citizen army finds a new courage, a new and violent energy. In the theatre we are presented with a second battle scene, a second episode of exhilarating action. This time it brings success, and it is followed by one of the most remarkable passages in the play: 'The Volsces fly, and Martius follows them to the gates, and is shut in.' The hero is alone in the enemy city.

It is clear that we are not meant to witness this scene but to imagine it. The speech of the First Soldier tells us that the Volsces have 'clapped to their gates', and what happens transpires behind closed doors. This is a superbly effective dramatic device and has its repercussions on the whole of the subsequent action. What we are required to envisage is a man capturing a city single-handed. This is the very stuff of heroism, but by having us imagine it (after already presenting us with two scenes of violent conflict) Shakespeare avoids staging what could so easily be merely crass. Instead we are encouraged into awe and admiration tinged with the thrilling doubt as to whether the hero will emerge alive or not.

29

As stagecraft – as the creation of suspense – this is excellent. It is also profoundly suggestive. Ordinary men like the two soldiers who refuse to follow Martius are incapable of such deeds. The hero, however, moves out of our sight and into a realm of warfare and carnage that has something ineluctably mysterious about it. The superman, the god of war, is all the more powerful for being invisible, imagined.

Above all, he is alone. The greatness of this soldier is unique. It sets him apart from other men and, in so doing, it imposes on him the terrible isolation of supreme ability. Any relationship such a man can have with his fellows must to some degree be a compromise with their limitations. And Caius Martius cannot compromise, cannot lessen and besmirch the military excellence, the horror and the awesomeness of what is happening behind those closed city gates.

Such an action cannot take place in a void, and Shakespeare brilliantly contrasts suspense and Caius Martius' eventual triumph to misplaced grief. The entire army has to express the emotion conveyed by the line 'Slain, sir, doubtless.' They are united in a common sadness at the supposed death of the man who is at once their hero and their scourge. Such simple, communal expressions have a very powerful effect, and they are followed by Lartius' equally powerful speech. This is an elegy for a great soldier, a tribute to military excellence. It is rhetoric at its finest:

> Thou art lost, Martius.
> A carbuncle entire, as big as thou art,
> Were not so rich a jewel. Thou wast a soldier
> Even to Cato's wish, not fierce and terrible
> Only in strokes, but with thy grim looks and
> The thunder-like percussion of thy sounds
> Thou mad'st thine enemies shake, as if the world
> Were feverous and did tremble.

> (I.iv.56–63)

The stature of the hero and his worth to the community could hardly be made more nobly clear. The reappearance of the living Martius, covered in blood and fighting the enemy, is thereby made all the more amazing and welcome. Communal joy raises new energies and we are presented with a third vivid military encounter: 'They fight, and all enter the city.' Rome and *romanitas* have triumphed.

Act I scene v

The small incident of the Roman soldiers with their spoils again shows Shakespeare's stagecraft at its most refined. We have now seen or imagined the hero in four military encounters and sensed something superhuman about him. These wretched men are his complete antithesis. The baseness of the Citizens is once again suggested and is underlined by Caius Martius' virulent contempt. By placing such an incident at this point Shakespeare not only creates an excellent sense of verisimilitude but provides the relief of contrast before showing his hero in yet another mighty encounter.

The Roman forces commanded by Cominius are, we know, under attack from Tullus Aufidius himself. The two great rivals must meet, and so important is this encounter that Shakespeare deliberately delays it and instead builds up yet further our sense of Martius' excellence. His seemingly inexhaustible physical energy and his courteous exchanges with his peers alike suggest the excellence of the aristocratic hero as he leaves to assist Cominius.

Act I scene vi

A skilful employment of contrast again gives life to the ensuing passages. Cominius' speech, for example, portrays him as a dignified and competent soldier but one who, unlike the hero, is suffering a temporary setback. Similarly the somewhat timid self-preservation of the Messenger is sharply contrasted to the sudden appearance of Martius covered in blood.

The ensuing dialogue, and Martius' constant attempts to speed the action, admirably convey the sense of a lull in a continuing military engagement. Aristocratic compliments are again juxtaposed to the hero's contempt for the common people, but after Martius has shown his generalship by asking questions about the disposition of the enemy, we are returned to the central issue of his conflict with Tullus Aufidius.

Martius implores Cominius to allow him to confront his great rival immediately. To the abundant heroism we have already seen is now added that personal emotion that runs so deeply in Martius' personality. The hero's enthusiasm (once again issuing in inspiring speech) wins him a band of willing followers. In sharp contrast to the opening scenes of the play, we see the Citizens united in patriotic exultation: 'They all shout and wave their swords, take him up in their arms, and cast up their caps.'

This is a tableau of great power. The language of such enthusiasm has no complicated grammar or syntax, but the shouting is a very powerful use of language, an expression of intense communal loyalty. We should, of course, contrast it both to the shouts of the mob at the start of the play and the 'voices' that are manipulated later on. Shakespeare's use of the chorus of Citizens is a device rich and subtle in both dramatic and thematic terms. Martius himself is exultant, but even as the troops lift him above their heads so he becomes isolated in the splendour they are, for the moment, acknowledging. His own comments reinforce this: 'O'me alone, make you a sword of me.' In his unique and solitary magnificence the hero imagines himself as no more a man. He exits in triumph, leading his loyal soldiers.

Act I scenes vii and viii

The brief scene in the Volsces' city again provides an effective pause before the encounter of the hero with his great rival. The scene which follows, added by Shakespeare to Plutarch's narrative, is of great interest both structurally and in terms of the play's themes.

As they meet, the two men exchange ritual abuse; for the moment their words are swords. Then they fall to action: 'Here they fight, and certain Volsces come in the aid of Aufidius. Martius fights till they be driven in breathless.' This is a complex and important moment in the play. We have thus far been encouraged to see both men in terms of aristocratic honour; a duel such as this is one of the principal methods of displaying that honour. What we are presented with, however, is its very opposite. Tullus Aufidius disgraces the code in his 'condemnèd seconds'. He reveals himself as treacherous, dishonourable, a machiavellian opportunist whose cynicism is in complete contrast to Martius' behaviour.

That Martius here secures a victory over his enemy is a tribute to his valour. It is yet another successful encounter in a day of extraordinary heroism. However, we are offered a vitally important insight into the nature of Tullus Aufidius and a superbly fashioned structural irony. In the first meeting between these two great rivals, Tullus Aufidius is shown using aides in his attempt to destroy his enemy. This attempt fails. In their last encounter, Aufidius will again ambush Martius. This time the hero will lie dead at his feet.

Act I scene ix

The end of scene viii creates an effective hiatus, and, after the sounding of the retreat, Shakespeare regroups the triumphant Romans for an important scene of what initially appears as public celebration. After successful action comes the language of praise.

Cominius' speech to Martius at the start of the scene sets this tone of
glowing public recognition, of what the rhetoricians called demonstrative, or epideictic, oratory. This will reach its climax in Cominius'
speech to the Senate in Act II scene ii. Just as much as valour and
matronly virtue, this grand public language was an aspect of *romanitas*.
Cominius himself gives a vivid description of a rhetorical culture where
great deeds are matched by great words:

> ... I'll report it
> Where senators shall mingle tears with smiles;
> Where great patricians shall attend and shrug,
> I'th'end admire; where ladies shall be frighted
> And, gladly quaked, hear more; where the dull tribunes,
> That with the fusty plebeians hate thine honours,
> Shall say against their hearts 'We thank the gods
> Our Rome hath such a soldier.'
>
> (I.ix.2–9)

This is a profoundly imaginative re-creation of a historical environment,
and the true note of triumph. Before Martius himself can reply to it,
however, Titus Lartius enters and begins a second encomium, or
speech of praise. The hero interrupts him:

> Pray now, no more. My mother,
> Who has a charter to extol her blood,
> When she does praise me grieves me. I have done
> As you have done – that's what I can; induced
> As you have been – that's for my country.
> He that has but effected his good will
> Hath overta'en mine act.
>
> (I.ix.13–19)

This has all the appearance of the modesty becoming a great gentleman,
and for the moment we may accept it as such. Cominius, however,
points out that great deeds are lost in silence – language is their
necessary accompaniment. His speech just hints at a false modesty in
the hero, and Cominius begs Martius to let him praise him before the
army as a 'sign of what you are'.

Language defines the man. It is an expression of his very being, his
identity. As we have seen, however, Martius believes his identity is most
fully revealed in his actions, in his military prowess, and once again he
tries to evade a speech of praise. We might begin to think that such
ostentatious modesty is close to pride and begin to see how Martius'
refusal to be praised exiles him from the community, of which speech
itself is one of the most important bonds.

Martius also refuses to accept the tenth of the spoils that are offered him, placing himself instead on the level of the common soldiers. He wins for this their immediate admiration: 'A long flourish. They all cry "Martius! Martius!", cast up their caps and lances.' Once again we have the public language of shouted approbation – the true response to a true hero. Plutarch's comment on this is interesting:

The soldiers, hearing Martius' words, made a marvellous great shout among them: and there were more that wondered at his great contentation and abstinence, when they saw so little covetousness in him, than there were that highly praised and extolled his valiantness. For even they themselves, that did somewhat malice and envy his glory, to see him thus honoured and passingly praised, did think him so much the more worthy of an honourable recompense for his valiant service, as the more carelessly he refused the great offer made unto him for his profit: and they esteemed more the virtue that was in him, that made him refuse such rewards, than that which made them to be offered to him, as unto a worthy person.

The speech that follows this public acclaim is entirely of Shakespeare's devising and reinforces the suggestions of the hero's haughty and embittered pride hinted at before. The language of modesty is swept aside by a torrent of virulent imagery reminiscent of the malcontent of contemporary satire. Martius shouts for silence. He commands an end to the language of praise. Drums, trumpets and steel are, for the soldier, the only honest sounds. Language, by comparison, is 'false-faced soothing', something intimately connected with 'lies'.

Cominius overrules him and takes the initiative into his own hands. He commands that Martius be given both a generous reward and a new name:

> For what he did before Corioles, call him
> With all th'applause and clamour of the host,
> Caius Martius Coriolanus.

(I.ix.62–4)

In the moment of his triumph the hero is given a new appellation. That most personal and suggestive of all words – the name – associates him with the enemy to whom he will later desert. For the moment, the 'son of Mars' is also 'Coriolanus'. It is a new and deeply ambivalent identity. Once again the soldiers loudly acclaim him.

There then follows the touching incident of Coriolanus's begging for mercy for a poor man of the Volsce city. This serves a double purpose. On the one hand we see a genuine effort at truly noble behaviour. On the other hand, the fact that Coriolanus forgets the man's name means that the man himself loses his identity. Names are an all-important index of existence, and the ironies attending the newly named hero are subtly underlined.

Act I scene x

As the victorious Romans go to their tents, the last scene of the *epitasis* presents us with their crestfallen enemies. Aufidius' speech shows that in defeat he too feels that he has lost his identity: 'I cannot,/Being a Volsce, be that I am.' In his despondency, he renounces honour. Politics and warfare are now to be conducted, by Aufidius at least, with a complete lack of scruple. In this, and in Coriolanus's own proud refusal to be at one with the standards of his community, lie the seeds of tragedy.

Catastasis

Thirdly, the Catastasis, [or] *counter-turn, which destroys that expectation, imbroils the action in new difficulties, and leaves you far distant from that hope in which it found you, as you may have observed in a violent stream resisted by a narrow passage; it runs round to an eddy, and carries back the waters with more swiftness than it brought them on.*

Dryden: Of Dramatic Poesy

Act II scene i

The central section of *Coriolanus*, the passage running from the hero's triumphal return to his ignominious exile from Rome, is one of the great achievements of Renaissance political drama. Here Shakespeare creates an extraordinarily full and complex picture of a society divided against itself and, in its fury, threatening its own destruction. The whole is centred around a vivid depiction of the abuse of language and the manipulation of action. The central issues of the play thus reach a new height of development.

The opening exchanges between Menenius and the Tribunes again establish the mood of conflict, while the relatively relaxed pace and witty alternations of abuse succeed in changing the tempo after the excited passages of action we have just witnessed.

Martius is again the subject of the conversation. Defining the nature of the hero is once more a central preoccupation. His wolfishness and pride are suggested, along with the enmity against him harboured by the people.

Menenius himself appears in his familiar role as the self-indulgent if quick-witted aristocrat able to out-manoeuvre his rivals through raillery. His contempt for the Tribunes – the contempt of a spokesman of the aristocracy for these newly appointed spokesmen of the people – reinforces the sense of social division in Rome. Factionalism now becomes a matter for satire, the contempt of those of the 'right-hand file' for political jobbery:

You know neither me, yourselves, nor any thing. You are ambitious for poor knaves' caps and legs. You wear out a good wholesome forenoon in hearing a cause between an orange-wife and a faucet-seller, and then rejourn the controversy of threepence to a second day of audience. When you are hearing a matter between party and party, if you chance to be pinched with the colic, you make faces like mummers, set up the bloody flag against all patience, and, in roaring for a chamber-pot, dismiss the controversy bleeding, the more entangled by your hearing. All the peace you make in their cause is calling both the parties knaves. (II.i.63–74)

A new and vivid level of language has been introduced to the play, the quickly moving and highly specific language of Shakespeare's comic prose. It is a language which creates a world of everyday incident. We are at once a long way from the high rhetoric of *romanitas* and the battlefield.

We are still, however, very close to the main themes of the play. The power of language remains a major concern. Here, Menenius is showing its abuse in the courts, the very centres of social justice. The incompetence of the Tribunes – men, it seems, unable to efficiently conduct even the most trivial concerns of a magistrates' court – is vividly suggested. Wrangling, roaring and time-wasting leave the most petty cases more entangled than ever. The language of the law, of smooth social functioning, ends merely in abuse. The tribunes of the people, Menenius suggests, have no effective control of even the most minor elements of social cohesion. The implication is that to trust them with real power would be to invite chaos.

With the entry of the three Roman matrons, Menenius at once turns to the language of aristocratic compliment. Social distinctions are again made evident through speech. Volumnia's announcement that Martius is coming home gives a new excitement to the action. In place of orange sellers and chamber-pots, we hear about wounds and oak garlands. These symbols of military prestige enhance the hero's status and, for the aristocrats at least, seem to promise new health and cohesion for the city. Volumnia and Menenius count up Martius' twenty-seven wounds with the enthusiasm of people describing a patriotic fetish object.

A flourish of trumpets (those crucial sound effects in the play) heralds the approach of the hero himself, while Volumnia's speech carries with it suggestions of a terrible and ruthless power:

> These are the ushers of Martius. Before him
> he carries noise, and behind him he leaves tears.

37

> Death, that dark spirit, in's nervy arm doth lie,
> Which, being advanced, declines, and then men die.
>
> (II.i.151–4)

The triumphal entry of the hero is accompanied by images of dreadful foreboding. At the core of national celebration lies an ominous and primeval force of destruction.

The words of the Herald are a public language of praise and announce to the assembled company Martius' new and ambivalent addition to his name. As in the earlier part of the play, the effect of the repeated shouting of the title 'Coriolanus' is at once martial, patriotic and ambiguous. The enemy city is never far from our thoughts.

To this public celebration, however, Coriolanus at once juxtaposes his own disdain for the language of public praise. His extreme sensitivity to the power of language – and, more particularly, to its potential for abuse – is made clear from the moment of his entry into his city. Throughout the *catastasis*, this contempt will build into a matter of central concern. Here, the exile of the hero from the language that is the bond of his people is brought sharply into focus. Coriolanus already stands at a distance from the city that would honour him and from which, at the end of the *catastasis*, he will voluntarily exile himself.

The element of patrician disdain in Coriolanus's refusal to join in communal celebration is enhanced by the fact that, when he turns to speak to the three Roman matrons, both his language and his action display a deft courtesy. He kneels before his mother with words of gratitude and filial obedience. This, we may feel, is the true and poised bearing of the noble life, a life of custom and ceremony.

We should also be aware, however, that Coriolanus's behaviour suggests the excessive devotion to his mother and her noble family mentioned much earlier in the play. It symbolizes at once matters of emotional and social loyalty that are potentially destructive to the well-being of the commonwealth. It is also an ironic foretaste of the great scene at the climax of the *catastrophe* when the hero's mother kneels before her son and begs him to spare the city that has raised him.

It is only now, after greeting his mother, that Coriolanus turns to his 'gracious silence', his wife. The dominance of his mother over his other relationships is shrewdly made clear, while Menenius' welcome gives a final flourish to a scene of aristocratic patriotism and celebration. For these people, the honours of Rome belong to the 'good patricians'. Rome is once again seen to rest on an aristocratic basis.

Brutus seems to confirm that this aristocratic superiority is a natural force. His speech is a remarkable poetic evocation of a Roman triumph. The crowd of pressing details is wonderfully evoked: the nurse letting her baby cry as she dashes off to watch the celebration, the kitchen-maid honouring the scene with her tawdry finery, vestal virgins inching their way through the throng as every ledge fills with all manner of people. Such is the power of aristocratic excellence. We are made to feel that a whole city – its multifarious people and purposes – have all been focused on the single hero:

> Such a pother
> As if that whatsoever god who leads him
> Were slily crept into his human powers
> And gave him graceful posture.
>
> (II.i.210–13)

The 'son of Mars' reveals his true ancestry in his bearing. There is indeed a godlike power to Coriolanus, and its natural majesty, apparently assuring his election to the Senate, sets the political aspirations of the Tribunes at naught.

But if Coriolanus is in some respects a god, he is, in others, less than a man, less than a full member of the civic community. With his awesomeness goes the pride and lack of temperance that will be his undoing. Alone of all the city, the Tribunes batten on this weakness in order to be the first to exploit it. To achieve this they rely on the fickleness of the common people, their absolute inability to hold a consistent view. This, as we saw, was one of the accusations levelled at the Citizens by Coriolanus himself at the start of the work:

> Your virtue is
> To make him worthy whose offence subdues him
> And curse that justice did it. Who deserves greatness
> Deserves your hate; and your affections are
> A sick man's appetite, who desires most that
> Which would increase his evil. He that depends
> Upon your favours swims with fins of lead
> And hews down oaks with rushes.
>
> (I.i.172–9)

This commonplace of Renaissance political thought will soon be made vividly apparent. Language and action will be essential to its realization, and Brutus's words deftly remind the audience of the conditions they will exploit to achieve this.

In order to be elected to the consulship, Coriolanus must appear in

39

the market-place dressed in the 'napless vesture of humility'. He must show his wounds to the people and 'beg their stinking breaths'. In other words, Roman custom requires that he deny his true nature. He must appear in clothes symbolic of humility and 'beg' for the 'voices' or opinions of the very class he most despises and mistrusts. He must submit to an action and use a language that are wholly alien to his nature. But Coriolanus has given his 'word' that he will never do this. While he would be happy enough to take the consulship if the words of his own class – 'the suit of the gentry' – were sufficient to guarantee him his place, his pride is such that he would rather refuse the highest position his nation can offer him than submit to the judgement of the Citizen class. From this dilemma of language and action will spring ineluctable tragedy.

The Tribunes are certain they know how to exploit the situation. Meanwhile, the Messenger summons them to the Capitol, offering once again a suggestion of the power of words:

> I have seen the dumb men throng to see him and
> The blind to hear him speak.

(II.i.254–5)

We wait in anticipation for a unique display of the power of language.

Act II scene ii

The discussion between the First and Second Officers that opens the scene is an important prelude to it. These two nameless men (their voices, perhaps, suggesting a superior level of education to that of the rank and file of the Citizens) analyse the issues involved with an objectivity that helps direct the audience's own response.

The idea that Coriolanus is 'vengeance proud and loves not the common people' is made explicit, as is the fickle valuation of merit to be expected from the people. Indifference, the Second Officer suggests, should be the hero's proper response to this, and he expresses his own belief that Coriolanus's 'noble carelessness' – his aristocratic aloofness to common things – expresses just this mood.

The First Officer's response is more shrewd. He realizes that Coriolanus's attitude to the people is not indifference but an active animosity which, in its way, is quite as destructive as the Tribunes' attempt to woo the common people's favour for their own purposes: 'to seem to affect the malice and displeasure of the people is as bad as that which he dislikes – to flatter them for their love.'

Language that is motivated by personal and dishonest prejudice is an evil, whatever way it inclines. True language, on the other hand, is an honest response to actions in the real world. Great actions, the Second Officer suggests, have their own eloquence, and the words of men must be at one with these. Anything else is a form of deceit:

> . . . he hath so planted his honours in their eyes and his actions in their hearts that for their tongues to be silent and not confess so much were a kind of ingrateful injury. To report otherwise were a malice that, giving itself the lie, would pluck reproof and rebuke from every ear that heard it.   (II.ii.27–32)

This brief exchange provides us with values that are essential to the interpretation of what is to follow. We have been offered an ideal of language in which words are at one with deeds and so bind all men of goodwill into a harmonious community. This image of harmony will soon be reduced to grating dissonance, and with it will come the near destruction of Rome itself. For the moment, however, after the triumphal entry of the leaders of society into the Capitol, Menenius too urges the ideal of an honourable language that is at one with honourable deeds.

The First Senator urges Cominius to speak with true eloquence and requests the Tribunes to listen with their 'kindest ears'. Sicinius' response to this is a first and ragged breach in the ideal of a language that is at one with intention. His oily words are a lie. Neither he nor Brutus have hearts 'inclinable to honour'. The whole purpose of the assembly is a threat to their existence, while Brutus's retort raises the spectre of Coriolanus's pride – the discordant element that will soon wreck the harmony of Rome. He has to be quickly silenced by Menenius.

Coriolanus's response is to get up and begin to leave. We know that he feels the public recognition of his deeds to be a profound threat, that language is something in contradistinction to action:

> oft,
> When blows have made me stay, I fled from words.
> You soothed not, therefore hurt not. But your people,
> I love them as they weigh –
>
>   (II.ii.69–72)

Words make the man of action almost a coward, and his pride having forced what for him is an unbreachable distinction between language and action, he turns to abuse the people. Menenius is forced to silence him, to stop his torrent of words. Coriolanus, as a result, turns and walks out of the Capitol. He rejects the celebration of his patriotic deeds in the very centre of the public life of his nation. Proudly disparaging his own worth, he suggests that language – that uniquely human gift – creates only monsters, things that are inhuman. In a span of imagery that is of the greatest importance to the play, we see the hero associated both with gods, man's highest potential, and with beasts, the lowest level to which he may be degraded.

Meanwhile, Coriolanus's worth is explored in his absence. Cominius' ensuing speech is one of the great passages of Shakespearian rhetone, and it is proper to discuss it at least partly in rhetorical terms.

Cominius' earlier language and action have already established his *ethos*, those personal qualities which lend extra conviction to his speech. For the rhetoricians these qualities constituted one element of 'proof', or successful persuasion. Cominius then reinforces this sense of personal integrity by quietly deprecating his own abilities at the start of what he has to say. The use of such a 'modesty formula' was a recognized way of getting an audience well-disposed and attentive. Here is true rhetoric in action.

The gist of the speech is then given in a *sententia*, or maxim:

> It is held
> That valour is the chiefest virtue and
> Most dignifies the haver.
>
> (II.ii.81–3)

Shakespeare derived this almost word for word from Plutarch, who had written:

> Now in those days valiantness was honoured in Rome above all other virtues; which they call *virtus*, by the name of virtue itself, as including in that general name all other special virtues besides.

Cominius then uses the career of Coriolanus to illustrate this point, attempting thereby to show the hero as the personification of *romanitas*. We hear of the sixteen-year-old boy facing the forces of Tarquin, slaying three opposers and even tackling the last king of Rome himself. Such an enumeration of deeds was referred to as *demonstratio*, and energy (*energia*) was a desired rhetorical attribute of such a passage.

Images or 'colours' were regarded as particularly helpful here and Dryden, writing in full consciousness of the rhetorical tradition, was to define the essence of such heroic poetry as 'some lively and apt description, dressed in such colours of speech that it sets before your eyes the absent object as perfectly and more delightfully than nature'. This Cominius' speech achieves, and the images he uses are particularly interesting. He talks of the young Coriolanus's 'Amazonian chin' and then, with what would have been regarded as admirable artifice, provides the following passage:

> His pupil age
> Man-entered thus, he waxèd like a sea,
> And in the brunt of seventeen battles since
> He lurched all swords of the garland.
>
> (II.ii.96–9)

The idea that Coriolanus is both a boy and a man is kept subtly in view. So too are various other central features of the play's presentation of his character:

> He was a thing of blood, whose every motion
> Was timed with dying cries. Alone he entered
> The mortal gate of th'city, which he painted
> With shunless destiny; aidless came off,
> And with a sudden reinforcement struck
> Corioles like a planet.
>
> (II.ii.107–12)

Here is the war-machine, the 'thing of blood', glimpsed in his essential isolation. Destiny, uniqueness and death are all associated, and the cluster of images is completed by seeing the hero as a planet. The reference is clearly to Mars and to a city brought down by something approaching a supernatural force. The numinous elements in Coriolanus's personality are once again brought to the fore.

Two other qualities required of the orator – memory and delivery – were akin to the skills of the actor, and to appreciate the working of these in Cominius' speech we must envisage its performance on the stage.

All writers on rhetoric were agreed that a speech, while it should be the object of the most intense care and intellectual elaboration, should be delivered in a way that appeared spontaneous. The arrangement of the various parts of the oration, the factual details and the rhetorical embellishments, had to be presented in a manner that seemed wholly natural. This is certainly the effect achieved here. Cominius speaks without notes and with apparent spontaneity. What he says, however, is very carefully tailored to the persuasion of an aristocratic audience. His elaborately contrived effects have, we may suppose, been carefully committed to memory.

Effective delivery or *pronuntiatio* was also vitally important. Thomas Wilson makes this point clear in the *Arte of Rhetorique* through the use of an anecdote:

Demosthenes therefore, that famous orator, being asked what was the chiefest point in all oratory, gave the chief and only praise to pronunciation; being demanded what was the second, and the third, he still made answer pronunciation, and would make no other answer till they left asking, declaring hereby, that art without utterance can do nothing, utterance without can do much aright.

Voice control, and particularly the use of amplification, was essential for delivering such a speech as Cominius'. So, too, was the control of gesture. Rhetorical handbooks were sometimes accompanied by woodcut illustrations to guide the speaker in these matters, and the effective use of gesture reaches its climax in the tremendous moment in the *catastrophe* when Coriolanus's mother kneels before her son as she pleads for the life of her city. The actor playing Cominius should ensure that all of these rhetorical qualities are present in his speech. Humanist rhetoric and Jacobean stage practice are here at one.

At its close, Cominius' speech is greeted with the expected approbation. Coriolanus himself is once again summoned to appear before the patricians and a place in the Senate is offered him.

'It then remains/That you do speak to the people.' The prospect fills the hero with horror and he begs to be allowed to 'o'erleap that custom'. This is a serious matter. By hoping to place himself above convention, Coriolanus is also placing himself at variance with the traditions of his city. In an important way, he is denying his full *romanitas*. As the early Latin epic poet Ennius had written: *Antiquis moribus res, stat Romana virisque* ('By ancient and customary things, the Roman state stood firm').

By denying tradition, Coriolanus at once establishes the force of pride over convention and so wins the enmity of the Tribunes of the people. This is the opportunity they have been waiting for. The people must have their 'voices' – their chance to use language in the political process – but they are confronted by a hero who will not underline his self-evident worth through words. He will not readily subscribe to tradition. Menenius, as ever, tries to cover things up and encourages the Senators to drown potential dissent in loud acclamations. Once again, Coriolanus's ambiguous name is shouted loudly in public. The patricians then leave to a flourish of cornets.

Sicinius and Brutus are left behind, certain that if Coriolanus is forced to the market-place he will beg the people's favour in a manner which will deny the apparent import of his words. Passion and semantics will be at odds. The Tribunes, meanwhile, prepare to manipulate the 'voices' of the people. Language and action are being terribly wrested from direct and honest purposes.

Act II scene iii

The *seven or eight Citizens* who now appear on stage present us with a view of the democratic process at once jaundiced and bitterly comic, and it is important to realize that Shakespeare considerably altered his source at this point to develop his own political and dramatic purposes. In Plutarch, Coriolanus is not reluctant to appear before these people in the market-place, rather the reverse. He willingly shows them his wounds, and they then reluctantly declare: 'We must needs choose him Consul; there is no remedy.' A dawning realization that they have put 'sovereign authority into his hands', however, makes them soon repent, and 'the love and goodwill of the common people turned straight to an hate and envy toward him'. There is no mention of the Tribunes of the people.

In Shakespeare's play, the influence that an opportunist and cynical élite have over mass democratic forces is revealed with chilling insight. In the pursuit of power, language becomes a form of action – an action wholly corrupt – by which the fickleness of the people is exploited by men seeking office for its own sake. This scene of the play becomes the bleakest of meditations on democracy.

From the start the 'many-headed multitude' are shown to be proud of the power of their 'voices', but also as realizing that the circumstances are such that they can only in reason give their assent to the election of Coriolanus to the Senate. Confronted with the silent eloquence of the hero's known achievements, they have a power which is in reality no power. There is simply no room for political debate; their assent to his election must be automatic. Anything else would show them for what they are conventionally taken to be, and which the development of the scene will show that they truly are: a fickle body wholly unworthy of trust.

... if he show us his wounds and tell us his deeds, we are to put our tongues into those wounds and speak for them. So, if he tell us his noble deeds, we must also tell him our noble acceptance of them. Ingratitude is monstrous, and for the multitude to be ingrateful were to make a monster of the multitude; of the which we being members should bring ourselves to be monstrous members. (II.iii.5–12)

This is, of course, exactly what will happen, and once more the imagery in which it is discussed is important. The 'monstrous' is again mentioned. We are presented with a view of the politically bestial, of that which works against community – against kind, kindred and mankind. Ingratitude is one expression of this, and kindness and naturalness,

45

unkindness and unnaturalness, become increasingly important themes in the play.

When Coriolanus enters in the gown of humility, the magnificent body of the isolated hero is juxtaposed to the assembled diversity of the body politic. A fundamental confrontation is given vivid emblematic form. Language is the crucial means of uniting the two, and the words of the Third Citizen make this clear: 'He's to make his requests by particulars, wherein every one of us has a single honour, in giving him our own voices with our own tongues.'

The language of begging that Coriolanus sees as required of him reduces him to the fury of a man who feels his integrity to be deeply threatened. Why should he use words to ask for what he so patently deserves? For the hero, the entire ceremony is a cruel farce, and his bitter retorts to Menenius bring to the surface once again the fact that language forces him to compromise with unworthiness. Menenius, for his part, begs Coriolanus to speak in a 'wholesome manner', and then departs.

The first round of the election takes place with Coriolanus coldly disdainful of those from whom he must beg. The price of the consulship is 'to ask it kindly' – in other words, to request it in a way that unites the body politic. Coriolanus merely insists that he should have it of right. The Citizens, awed by his presence, by the dumb eloquence of his reputation, grant him the consulship, yet they immediately come to see that their 'voices' have worked to their own disadvantage. They realize they might well repent of their choice: 'An 'twere to give again – but 'tis no matter.'

Coriolanus's encounter with the Fourth and Fifth Citizens increases the tone of bitter disdain, his own utter contempt for the act he feels he is required to put on. It is perhaps the most telling measure of his belief that his proven worth is an intensely private and personal matter that he once again refuses to show his wounds in public: 'I will not seal your knowledge with showing them. I will make much of your voices and so trouble you no farther.' The emblems of real virtue remain hidden while language becomes further debased. In his fury and sarcasm Coriolanus becomes an adept at severing the surface meaning of language from the speaker's real feelings. The hero himself thus becomes crucially involved in language as deception:

> Most sweet voices!
> Better it is to die, better to starve,
> Than crave the hire which first we do deserve.

> Why in this wolvish toge should I stand here
> To beg of Hob and Dick that does appear
> Their needless vouches? Custom calls me to't.
> What custom wills, in all things should we do't,
> The dust on antique time would lie unswept
> And mountainous error be too highly heaped
> For truth to o'erpeer.

(II.iii.111–20)

But *romanitas* is largely based on custom, and for Coriolanus to deny its power is in part to exile himself from his community. His vindictiveness at this point already puts him in a kind of internal exile from the state he serves. Soon this exile will become an established fact.

Menenius now comes in to save him from further degradation. Coriolanus has stood his required time in the market-place. All that remains now is an apparent formality: the process of his confirmation in the consulship. The 'custom of request' has been discharged – albeit in a way that will lead to its being rendered invalid – and the patrician party can now return to the Senate House, their duty apparently done.

When Brutus and Sicinius are left alone with the people, the divide between language and intention already made so dramatically evident is widened into a gulf that threatens the utmost political danger, a rift which threatens to swallow the entire state.

'He mocked us when he begged our voices.' Coriolanus has divorced words from emotional sincerity. Now the 'voices' begin openly to repent of their choice. They reveal themselves indeed as the expression of the 'many-headed multitude', people incapable of true valuation or constant opinions. Their own representatives berate them for their 'childish' conduct.

In so doing the Tribunes also reveal a bitter irony. The infantile and fickle Citizens had apparently been earlier 'lessoned' by their masters into the response they should have given. This is the first time the audience hears about this. We did not know that the 'seven or eight Citizens' who appeared at the start of the scene had in fact had their 'voices' trained for them. In retrospect, the fact that they were so impressed by the mere physical presence of Coriolanus (despite the embittered cynicism of his language) makes the numinous and almost godlike power with which he is invested seem all the more mighty. The people, by contrast, seem to be even more fickle; they have accepted the Tribunes' instructions and then rejected them. Now they wish they had followed them. Such people, it could reasonably be supposed, may be influenced to any end.

The Tribunes continue to berate the people for their folly in not following instructions and, in so doing, they craftily exploit their power as demagogues. The Citizens, humiliated by the revelation of the worthlessness of their voices, resort to violence. Voices that once flattered themselves that they had the power of individual choice now resort to the fury of the mob. The collective voice is assembled to scream its denunciation of the man the people have just chosen to be their master:

THIRD CITIZEN	He's not confirmed; we may deny him yet.
SECOND CITIZEN	And will deny him.
	I'll have five hundred voices of that sound.
FIRST CITIZEN	I twice five hundred, and their friends to piece 'em.

(II.iii.208–11)

Language – the Citizens' voices – has become an expression of anarchy. In this world where order has been turned upside down, lies become the instruments of power. The Tribunes, delighting in the fecundity of their own cynicism, urge the people to lay the 'fault' of Coriolanus's election on them:

> Say we read lectures to you,
> How youngly he began to serve his country,
> How long continued, and what stock he springs of . . .
>
> (II.iii.234–6)

Coriolanus's very real merits, the elements in his personality that the Tribunes were so keen to play down, now become the means of working the hero's downfall. Revelling in their demagoguery, the Tribunes urge the Citizens to assert that they have been led astray by their own leaders. With language so chaotically divided from the truth, 'mutiny' is about to fall on the state.

Act III scene i

With Rome divided against itself, the threats from the enemy without are added to the threats from the enemy within: we learn that Tullus Aufidius has reassembled his forces. Coriolanus is immediately fascinated by the mention of his great rival's name. The personal again becomes a guiding force in his activity, and he eagerly questions Titus Lartius as to whether Aufidius has mentioned him. He is told that he has and that combat between them is the one thing Aufidius most looks forward to. Coriolanus relishes a similar ambition and, with bitter irony, wishes he had a reason to seek Aufidius in his city of Antium. Very soon he will have one.

Mention of war against the Volsces is immediately lost in the civil broils that are wrenching the Roman state apart. Sicinius and Brutus, confident of the might of the Citizens' voices, bar the hero's way. Told that he has not, in fact, been elected consul by the people, Coriolanus immediately despises their fickle voices and realizes that there is a plot afoot to 'curb the will of the nobility'.

Menenius fails to check the hero's mounting fury, and, as Brutus begins to taunt him, Coriolanus's anger increases. We feel his fury straining at the curbs his fellow patricians try to place on it. Language itself becomes barely restrained violence, and eventually it breaks out in an extreme assertion of the necessity for hierarchy and aristocratic rule. The hero 'coins words' with reckless abandon as he portrays his absolute and divisive image of the state. This is language unchecked by the intellect. As Menenius later declares:

> His heart's his mouth.
> What his breast forges, that his tongue must vent,
> And, being angry, does forget that ever
> He heard the name of death.
>
> (III.i.256–9)

Unpremeditated violence of speech is seen as a denial of humanity. It is reckless, destructive and ultimately fatal. It divides the community against itself and leads inevitably to tragedy. Its force is at once terrifying and anarchic, and it builds here to an ever more brutal crescendo. Against the unbridled shouting of the mob, Shakespeare juxtaposes the unbounded pride and fury of Coriolanus himself. Embattled speech becomes civil war. The ineffective efforts of the patricians to control their figurehead as he pours out his wrath in a torrent of words enhance the sense that this newly elected consul is working anarchy in the state.

The Tribunes slyly exploit the situation, Sicinius urging Coriolanus's arrest. Violence and confusion break out in the heart of Rome, and the stage becomes an emblem of a community tearing itself apart.

Menenius is caught between the violence of Coriolanus and the rabble-rousing of the Tribunes. And while these two sides hurl abuse and inflammatory comments, the united voice of the Citizens also roars its opinion. In a play so intimately concerned with language, the sheer cacophony at this point is its own terrible comment on what is happening. Matters reach a climax as Coriolanus, now condemned to death by the voices of the people, draws his sword against the inhabitants of his own city. This is a terrible foreshadowing of what is to come.

For the moment, however, the patricians have the upper hand: 'In this mutiny the Tribunes, the Aediles, and the people are beat in.' None the less, for the aristocratic party this is a pyrrhic victory. The best they can do is to try to usher their hero off the stage and away from language and action altogether.

The violent language of the chief representative of the patrician party has put his own side in peril while threatening to undermine the state itself. The Tribunes again demand Coriolanus's death – the death of the one man who can lead them against their stirring enemy – while Menenius, as always, is obliged to try and patch up such a compromise as he can. In the face of the mounting fury of the Tribunes, he urges that they proceed by 'process', by the due forms of law. To permit anything else would be to capitulate to the anarchic forces of the mob. Roman institutions must be given a chance to save a Roman hero whose very excesses measure both the greatness and the limitations of aristocratic *romanitas*:

> Consider this. He has been bred i'th'wars
> Since 'a could draw a sword, and is ill schooled
> In bolted language. Meal and bran together
> He throws without distinction. Give me leave,
> I'll go to him and undertake to bring him
> Where he shall answer by a lawful form,
> In peace, to his utmost peril.
>
> (III.i.318–24)

A man incapable of 'bolted language' has, by the violence of his unpremeditated words, brought himself to the position where his true patriotism and worth to the community must be tested by the word of law. The man so recently elected consul is now on trial for his life.

Act III scene ii

Coriolanus's own words have wrought him near to the pitch of self-destructive anger. His violent assertions, his virulent language of pride and honour, have made him a man almost wholly divorced from civil existence. He is surprised that his mother – for him the very embodiment of what he believes to be the patrician ideal of *romanitas* – appears not fully to approve of him.

With the entry of Volumnia, however, the 'boy' has to begin to learn a greater political pragmatism, a worldly-wise equivocation that is wholly opposed to his natural and untutored instincts:

> Pray be counselled.
> I have a heart as little apt as yours,
> But yet a brain that leads my use of anger
> To better vantage.
>
> (III.ii.28–31)

What Volumnia is suggesting is that the values shared by both mother and son – the ideals of patrician Rome – are not to be maintained by their mere assertion, but by political manipulation, requiring above all the manipulation of words. We have already seen the acute distaste which sundering the meaning of words from their underlying intentions inspires in Coriolanus. His magnificent, if frighteningly naïve, integrity is horrified by 'bolted language'. Now, however, his esteemed mother (drawing a shrewd parallel with military tactics) obliges him to just such deceit. She tells him he must defend himself in the market-place not by a spontaneous torrent of abuse motivated by a sense of personal honour, but by guile.

Honour must be maintained by dishonourable means. Words must be deliberately twisted, intention and semantics divorced. To Coriolanus this is a horrifying prospect, but Volumnia's speech offers a most important insight into the nature of purely political language, language as power and self-preservation in the cynical market-place of the world:

> . . . it lies you on to speak
> To th'people, not by your own instruction,
> Nor by th'matter which your heart prompts you,
> But with such words that are but roted in
> Your tongue, though but bastards and syllables
> Of no allowance to your bosom's truth.
> Now this no more dishonours you at all
> Than to take in a town with gentle words,
> Which else would put you to much fortune and
> The hazard of much blood.
> I would dissemble with my nature where
> My fortunes and my friends at stake required
> I should do so in honour.
>
> (III.ii.52–64)

He who most shrewdly manipulates language has power. Mere honour asserted with whatever force is of no value in the political world. Volumnia, we feel, has read the great cynics of Renaissance politics; she

51

has studied her Machiavelli and Francis Bacon and has learned the appalling truth that language was given to man to disguise his thoughts.

She also knows, as every orator knew, that 'Action is eloquence.' Her lesson in rhetoric as deceit proceeds apace. Having taught her son the advantages of 'bolted language', Volumnia now instructs him in other aspects of eloquence, in particular the art of gesture. With what we may perhaps assume is the exaggerated emphasis of the teacher, she shows her son how to kneel before his audience, how to move his head up and down as a sign of repentance, and how to beat his breast. Then, having offered such a fine performance of sophisticated rhetorical deceit, he is – with a beoming 'modesty formula' – to declare he is only a soldier, a man unused to speaking in the 'soft way'. Such effects are bound to win over his audience. Like every orator, Coriolanus is to become an actor. The performance is all.

It is notable that during this comparatively long passage Coriolanus himself is silent. This is perhaps the most eloquent of comments on his being forced to mangle his integrity in the pursuit of political survival. When he does speak, it is to express his barely disguised mortification:

> Must I
> With my base tongue give to my noble heart
> A lie that it must bear?

> (III.ii.99–101)

There is great pathos in watching this man of undoubted integrity forced to sully himself with the world's values and teach his mind 'a most inherent baseness'. The price of civil survival, it seems, is compromise, dishonesty and deceitful language. But its opposite is Coriolanus's naïve and destructive assertion of values too great for the world to live with. It is a truly tragic paradox. The dutiful son consents to speak 'mildly' none the less. His survival depends on it, yet we know that in many respects it will be a diminished existence if Coriolanus agrees to a language of lies and duplicitous actions.

Act III scene iii

The Tribunes make sure that speaking 'mildly' is an impossibility, and their efforts offer a powerfully unillusioned insight into the public and political manipulation of language.

Having established the basis of their charge against Coriolanus – their belief that he 'affects Tyrannical power', despises the people and has refused to distribute 'the spoil got on the Antiates' – the Tribunes then show their skilful management of the Citizens. A list of their 'voices' has been prepared and the people themselves collected by 'tribes'. Sicinius then reveals how the common voice is to be orchestrated:

> Assemble presently the people hither.
> And when they hear me say 'It shall be so
> I'th'right and strength o'th'commons' be it either
> For death, for fine, or banishment, then let them,
> If I say 'Fine', cry 'Fine!', if 'Death', cry 'Death!'
> Insisting on the old prerogative
> And power i'th'truth o'th'cause.
>
> (III.iii.12–18)

Language and action are both subject to skilful political manipulation, the careful management of mob rule. The Tribunes think to secure their position by ensuring that as much noise as possible is raised, and to further their aim they plan to put Coriolanus himself 'to choler straight'. In other words, they will manipulate the hero into bursting forth with the torrent of abuse they know they can so easily stimulate. They will then use the shouting of the mob to exploit a reckless use of language. Politics is being conducted in a forum where language and reason have been almost completely separated.

At first, Coriolanus tries to preserve the discretion urged on him by his peers. His opening speech makes large patriotic gestures and his questions seem controlled and reasonable. Even when Sicinius insists that he submit himself to the people's voices – in effect to be tried in a people's court – he replies 'I am content.' Menenius tries to build on this advantage by asking the Citizens to consider that as a great soldier it is part of his nature to speak roughly.

The Tribunes then explain the charge they are levying against him:

> We charge you that you have contrived to take
> From Rome all seasoned office and to wind
> Yourself into a power tyrannical,
> For which you are a traitor to the people.
>
> (III.iii.63–6)

Demagogues who are trying to establish their own supremacy charge the national hero with being a tyrant. Worse, they accuse him of being a 'traitor'. That one word, a word which pierces to the very core of Coriolanus's being, pulls down the patricians' whole elaborate artifice of verbal manipulation. The hero's reckless integrity, baited beyond endurance, pours forth in the torrent of abuse the Tribunes had hoped for. For them, Coriolanus has condemned himself out of his own mouth. His words have wrought his own destruction, and the people howl for his death.

The Tribunes, however, seek to work a further refinement. Because of the 'service' he has done the state, they attempt to lighten Coriolanus's sentence from death to banishment. He has risen, however, to a magnificence of embittered fury in which the politics of 'bolted language' has no role:

> Let them pronounce the steep Tarpeian death,
> Vagabond exile, flaying, pent to linger
> But with a grain a day, I would not buy
> Their mercy at the price of one fair word,
> Nor check my courage for what they can give,
> To have't with saying 'Good morrow'.
>
> (III.iii.88–93)

By refusing language, Coriolanus has effectively exiled himself from his corrupt community. Now, to the approving roars of the Citizens, the sentence of exile is passed on him. Though Cominius tries to intercede, Brutus renders his plea useless as the Citizens continue their roaring. The law, such as it is, has had its say. There remains for its victim only one final form of language: the curse.

> You common cry of curs, whose breath I hate
> As reek o'th'rotten fens, whose loves I prize
> As the dead carcasses of unburied men
> That do corrupt my air – I banish you.
> And here remain with your uncertainty!
> Let every feeble rumour shake your hearts;
> Your enemies, with nodding of their plumes,
> Fan you into despair! Have the power still
> To banish your defenders, till at length
> Your ignorance – which finds not till it feels,
> Making but reservation of yourselves
> Still your own foes – deliver you
> As most abated captives to some nation
> That won you without blows! Despising
> For you the city, thus I turn my back.
> There is a world elsewhere.
>
> (III.iii.120–35)

This outburst of hideously destructive language is at once an emotional release and a summation of the thunderous abuse Coriolanus has directed at the plebeians since his first entry on to the stage.

It has its own terrible logic. Throughout the play, language – which should be the bond of the civil community – has been used as an instrument to tear it apart. In the strife of manipulated words, only Coriolanus among the major characters has tried (sometimes unsuccessfully, as in his ordeal in the market-place) to preserve the ideal of a speech in which language and intention are one. But this untutored and naïve language, if it is an expression of a patrician soldier's excellence, is also a weapon that wreaks hideous social division.

It is a language wholly lacking in temperance and any desire to bind the commonwealth into a united state. It is the summation of a purely partisan excellence which, asserted to its extreme, divides its speaker from a full participation in the life of the community. If its moral roots are excellence and honour, its social foundations are class and class warfare. Its virtues threaten the very community that gives rise to it. This is behaviour at once magnificent and abominable. And, as is the language, so is its speaker.

The logic of Coriolanus's position has now reached a terrible climax. The man whose language helped to divide his city and to separate him from its full and complex functioning now passes on himself the sentence of exile – the divorce from his community which has been all along implicit in his language. Paradox becomes tragic self-contradiction. The hero is both superb and contemptible, both the embodiment of an ideal of honour which the corrupt Tribunes refuse to recognize and the traitor they have declared him to be. Most pitifully of all, Coriolanus himself believes 'There is a world elsewhere'. There is not. There are no fresh starts.

Act IV scene i

After the vulgar triumph of the Tribunes and the people, the scene of Coriolanus's farewell to his family and friends has a heroic pathos which deepens the audience's response in important ways.

Contrast and thematic unity again provide the dramatic interest. A public scene full of vehement, destructive and manipulated language is followed by an intimate, domestic passage of grief. Coriolanus himself reveals a new tenderness and dignified humanity while, in a play so profoundly concerned with words, he uses the maxims his mother taught him in an attempt to raise her spirits. But these are to no avail; Volumnia can now only vent her emotions in curses.

Coriolanus's long speech repeats the idea of his own resilience triumphing over circumstances, while his courtesy and tenderness to his friends reveal a depth of emotion that helps to build pathos. The conclusion of the speech is none the less full of tragic irony:

> My mother, you wot well
> My hazards still have been your solace, and
> Believe't not lightly – though I go alone,
> Like to a lonely dragon that his fen
> Makes feared and talked of more than seen – your son
> Will or exceed the common or be caught
> With cautelous baits and practice.

(IV.i.27–33)

The extreme importance of Volumnia to her son's emotional life is reinforced, and this will be a factor of great importance to the *catastrophe*. Heroic effort is also suggested and, along with it, the isolation that we have seen to be an essential element in Coriolanus's magnificence.

The 'dragon', however, adds an important note. Such isolation as Coriolanus will now endure has something cruel and destructive in it that makes it less than human. We may also care to remember that Aristotle had declared that only a man or a god can live on its own, self-sufficiently. The Coriolanus we will now see is both bestial and the 'son of Mars', both animal and godlike. Such potential will either give rise to extremes of heroism or – an awful ironic indication of what will actually happen – be tricked and destroyed in the duplicitous world of men.

We thus see the hero as both magnanimous and isolated. Neither friends nor family can accompany him into the exile into which his greatness has thrust him. We are made aware both of the bonds of nature and of the man who has been obliged to sever himself from these.

Act IV scene ii

While they appear to have won the day, the Tribunes are aware that they must be careful in their handling of the people. They also realize that they have earned the hostility of the patricians. This last is made particularly clear as they encounter Volumnia, Virgilia and Menenius.

Ridiculously, the Tribunes try to flee from Volumnia. The edge of comedy makes them absurd while also suggesting that Volumnia's outbursts are mere unbridled female emotion, a matter of no account. She none the less manages to draw a particularly savage contrast between the Tribunes' manipulation of words and her son's exploits, between language and action. Coriolanus's heroism is thus kept constantly in view.

More importantly, the very ineffectiveness of the Roman matron's words at this point is in contrast to her effective use of language in the *catastrophe*. For the moment, the aristocratic party in Rome appears to be broken. The *catastasis* had opened with their triumph; it concludes with their defeat. The hero's reversal of fortune has been wrought with extreme dramatic skill and points towards the inexorable *catastrophe*.

Catastrophe

Lastly, the Catastrophe, *which the Grecians called* λύσις *['lusis'], the French* le dénouement, *and we the discovery or unravelling of the plot. There you see all things settling again upon their first foundations, and the obstacles which hindered the design or action of the play once removed, it ends with that resemblance of truth and nature that the audience are satisfied with the conduct of it.*

Dryden: Of Dramatic Poesy

Act IV scene iii

The *catastrophe* of the play centres around the hero's desertion to the enemy Volsces. Shakespeare's approach to this is indirect. Rather than opening with Coriolanus himself, he offers a meeting between a Roman and a Volsce spy in a scene which establishes the baseness of all treachery. 'I am a Roman; and my services are, as you are, against 'em.' This is the position soon to be adopted by Coriolanus himself.

The two spies are initially slow to recognize each other, and the emphasis laid on their names introduces a second theme of great importance to the play as a whole, and to the *catastrophe* in particular. The 'Coriolanus' who is about to desert to the enemy ranks also has his identity closely bound up with his borrowed name, and his use and eventual loss of it is crucial to the tragic climax.

This brief introductory scene also informs the audience about the political conditions pertaining in Rome after the hero's banishment. We discover that the Volsces already know about the 'strange insurrections' that have taken place there, but not about Coriolanus's actual banishment. Now, in addition to learning that 'a small thing' would make trouble flare up again between the patricians and the Tribunes, the Volsces discover that Rome has lost her greatest soldier. Both spies believe that Tullus Aufidius will now appear to advantage and, quite untroubled by their morally dubious roles, the two men accompany each other home. With the greatest dramatic economy, the opening scene of the *catastrophe* introduces a new mood to the play while developing some of its fundamental themes.

Act IV scene iv

Enter Coriolanus in mean apparel, disguised and muffled. The stage direction graphically describes Coriolanus's abject and essentially false state now he has deserted Rome, just as his speech (one of the hero's very few soliloquies) emphasizes his death-dealing nature:

> A goodly city is this Antium. City,
> 'Tis I that made thy widows. Many an heir
> Of these fair edifices 'fore my wars
> Have I heard groan and drop. Then know me not,
> Lest that thy wives with spits and boys with stones
> In puny battle slay me.
>
> (IV.iv.1–6)

The hero's military strength and the possibility of an ignominious death are suggested from the start.

Having been directed to the place where his great enemy is feasting his nobles before their attack on Rome, Coriolanus is given another soliloquy. It is a recklessly cynical expression of the instability of the bonds of human friendship. As the traitor enters the city of his enemy, he comments on the tiny incidents that break up all alliances. Both the tone of the speech and its failure to draw a truly adequate parallel with Coriolanus's own fate at this point suggest how confused his motives are. The hero's desertion is an act of will rather than an expression of his full and true nature. Through the sheer force of personality, this erstwhile personification of integrity is living a lie. None the less, the speech tragically foreshadows the violent changes of allegiance which will lead to his own death. Now, with reckless abandon, he enters the one place where he can perhaps forge an identity for himself:

> My birthplace hate I, and my love's upon
> This enemy town. I'll enter. If he slay me,
> He does fair justice. If he gives me way,
> I'll do his country service.
>
> (IV.iv.23–6)

This is the brutal cynicism of the desperate.

Act IV scene v

The first response of the Volsces is to turn him away because of his poor appearance. A quarrel immediately breaks out, and the comedy gives a particularly bitter edge to the importance of the themes that underlie it: the natural hostility of Volsce to Roman and plebeian to patrician, the isolation and danger that surround a nameless man, a man without an identity. Almost immediately on his arrival in the enemy city, a fight breaks out between Coriolanus and his erstwhile foes. Tullus Aufidius has to be summoned.

Identity, purpose, name and language suddenly become all-important. Tullus Aufidius demands to know who this man is who has interrupted his feast and thus violated the laws of hospitality. He asks the intruder no less than five times for his name. Eventually he is told:

> My name is Caius Martius, who hath done
> To thee particularly and to all the Volsces
> Great hurt and mischief; thereto witness may
> My surname, Coriolanus.

> (IV.v.68–71)

The hero's full name brings out the ambiguity of his situation. Caius Martius, the 'son of Mars', is the great soldier treacherously dealing with his enemy. The Roman who has acquired a name inseparable from an association with the Volsces – a name won in ravishing one of their towns – has now come to establish a new identity in the city of his foes. The hero himself is bitterly aware of the ironies here. His loyal service to his own country, the deeds which established his fame and sense of self, have been requited with a name that should strike hatred into the heart of the man he is now addressing. Of his old self, however, that name is all he has. 'Only that name remains.' His 'thankless country' has devoured the rest and ignominiously exiled him. He has come to Antium in 'mere spite'. All he can do is to offer his services to his enemy or be killed by him.

This very long speech from Coriolanus and Tullus Aufidius' almost equally lengthy reply serve several important dramatic purposes. This is their first major encounter, and it is vital to establish it on a different footing to the trickery and threats of revenge at any price that characterized Tullus Aufidius' fight with the hero at the close of the first act. While the memory of these cannot (and, indeed, must not) be wholly forgotten, the sheer length of Coriolanus's speech and its remarkable content allow the actor playing Tullus Aufidius time to suggest his developing reactions to an incredible situation. A fundamental ruthless enmity is glazed over with the warm admiration one great military man must necessarily feel for another. The element of friendship in rivalry comes to the fore and, with it, the feeling that Coriolanus may indeed find a new identity in the enemy city. Such cordiality, of course, makes the eventual betrayal of the hero all the more bitter and tragic.

For the moment, however, the complex nature of Tullus Aufidius' more positive feelings for Coriolanus is expressed. It is noticeable and, indeed, proper that he refers to him only as Martius. For Tullus Aufidius he is truly a 'son of Mars', or even the god himself. The intensity of his admiration could hardly be more evident, and it expresses itself in a warm embrace.

Too much can be made of the alleged homoerotic elements here. What Tullus feels is an admiration and identification as strong as sex, but which he is careful to distinguish from sex itself. It is a soldier's response to another fundamental human role: man as killer. His dreams of struggling with Martius operate in a similar way. The sexual drive as one of the strongest of human urges provides something of the imagery for portraying the desire to fight. What, with the most profound of ironies, emerges from this, however, is a vision of erstwhile enemies united:

> Worthy Martius,
> Had we no other quarrel else to Rome but that
> Thou art thence banished, we would muster all
> From twelve to seventy, and pouring war
> Into the bowels of ungrateful Rome,
> Like a bold flood o'erbear't. O, come, go in,
> And take our friendly senators by th'hands,
> Who now are here, taking their leaves of me
> Who am prepared against your territories,
> Though not for Rome itself.
>
> (IV.v.129–38)

The two rivals, united in a mutual admiration that will not, eventually, serve to disguise either the political or the personal divides it appears to hide, leave the stage together. Coriolanus has been welcomed into the city with a warmth previously unimaginable. The Servants tell of him sitting at the table with the Volsce senators, admired by Tullus Aufidius and treated as if 'he were son and heir to Mars'. His true nature has apparently been recognized.

But the Servants' dialogue carries other and equally subtle layers of implication. First of all, perhaps, the cowardliness and fickle opinions of these Volsce plebeians (an important element in the *catastrophe*) are made clear. Now that their master has become friends with the man they tried to expel, they imagine they realized his virtues all along. This is the changeability we have seen also from the Citizens of Rome, and

61

Shakespeare suggests that it is the characteristic of an entire class rather than merely of one national group.

The Servants' comparative physical weakness and their resulting admiration for Coriolanus's strength also witness to the sheer physical presence of the man. Most importantly of all, however, the Servants' dialogue immediately makes clear that comparisons between Coriolanus and Tullus Aufidius inevitably suggest competition and rivalry between the two men. For the moment, this is dealt with in a comic manner. It contains none the less, the seeds both of truth and unavoidable tragedy.

The path has now been prepared for war, a war all the more terrible for one of its leaders being a traitor. The dialogue of the Servants, however, is a comic and painful parody of the great soldiers' martial prowess. Peace is decried as a corrupting time which 'makes men hate one another'. War, by contrast is 'sprightly walking'. This is less cynicism than naïvety and is effective contrast to the very real terror that is about to descend on Rome.

Act IV scene vi

For the moment, though, Rome itself exists in a state of artificial peace. Sicinius declares that, with Coriolanus gone, tranquillity and friendship have returned to the city. The erstwhile unruly plebeians go happily about their business. Menenius is obliged to agree that this is so, yet he reaffirms the patrician view that things would have been even better if only Coriolanus had 'temporized', had been able to do the one thing he could not do, which was to compromise and so stay within the life of the community. The group of Citizens who now enter and greet the Tribunes again underline that peace has broken out in Rome, yet even this somewhat oily exchange cannot forbear to mention Coriolanus. Despite his exile, he is present in everyone's thoughts.

Suddenly he becomes a vivid threat. An Aedile (one of the officers of the law) enters to tell the Tribunes that the Volsces are preparing an attack. The audience is in the privileged position of knowing that Coriolanus is at the head of this. For the moment, however, Menenius can only point out to the Romans that such a threat would never have arisen if Coriolanus had not been banished. His role as the former defender of the city is suggested before the Romans learn that he is now their attacker.

The Tribunes refuse to believe the truth of what they have heard. The news is only a rumour, a false report, a lying use of words. They cannot imagine it possible that the Volsces should have broken their treaty with Rome. Coriolanus's speech on the rapid changes in human fortune and his own subsequent desertion to the Volsces have introduced the themes of treachery and sudden reversals of fortune into the play, however. Vulnerability – the foolishness of trusting to any lasting state of affairs – has been well established.

No sooner have the Tribunes ordered the bringer of bad news to be whipped than a second report confirms what he has said, adding to it the terrible information

> that Martius,
> Joined with Aufidius, leads a power 'gainst Rome,
> And vows revenge as spacious as between
> The young'st and oldest thing.
>
> (IV.vi.66–9)

Even Menenius cannot believe this; in his view such an alliance is against nature. But a second Messenger arrives to confirm the report, his language reinforcing the terror associated with the destroyer of his own city. Cominius the soldier immediately realizes the implications of what they have all been told and makes the assembled company realize, too, the full horror of what is about to befall them. The 'son of Mars' is about to make war on his own city:

> He is their god. He leads them like a thing
> Made by some other deity than Nature,
> That shapes man better; and they follow him
> Against us brats with no less confidence
> Than boys pursuing summer butterflies,
> Or butchers killing flies.
>
> (IV.vi.91–6)

The great soldier who has gone against nature has become a super-human and terrible force of destruction. The comprehensible order of the world has been destroyed, and the horrific image (familiar from *King Lear*) of the gods killing men for their sport becomes a political reality for the people of Rome. Not the least awful aspect of this is the fact that the Romans themselves – the Tribunes and the people especially – have been in large measure responsible for this. As representatives of the patricians, Cominius and Menenius turn on the men they feel are responsible for this horror. Their only hope is that 'the noble man' may have mercy.

But who can ask for it? How can any form of words possibly be appropriate? There is, it seems, no one in Rome who can speak for the city. Language is swallowed up in the inevitability of violence, a violence which the speeches of Cominius and Menenius make appear all the more terrible. Against the ghastly insights of their imaginations the Tribunes can only oppose the most futile of words: 'Say not we brought it.'

The frightened Citizens who now enter show immediately how cowardly and fluctuating their views are. Their ridiculous assertions that they thought they might have been wrong even while they were banishing Coriolanus are at once comic and pathetic – weak, unstable murmurs in a city about to be put to fire and the sword. 'Y'are goodly things, you voices!' The Tribunes try to contain their anxiety, but the scene has shifted from the expression of their cocky authority at the opening to a state of intense fear in which neither language nor action appears to have any chance of fending off inevitable destruction.

Act IV scene vii

The terror-inspiring greatness of Coriolanus – the success with which he acts out what is now his essentially false and unnatural role – is also in part the means of his destruction. Tullus Aufidius' admiration has once again turned to envy, and the scene in which he discusses the nature of his rival is one of the most interesting in the play.

The language of analysis is dense with imagery, knotted in its syntax and sometimes confused in expression. In a play so closely concerned with language, we feel that words themselves are trying to define a man whose greatness and limitations are, finally, beyond adequate description. The mystery of the divisive forces working within the hero are all the more powerful for their protean nature, and we shall see that Tullus Aufidius' own response to this is finally a devastating cynicism.

'Do they still fly to th'Roman?' The question contains a reluctant and jealous admission of the magnetic power of Coriolanus's magnificence. By associating this with the hero's nationality, however, Tullus Aufidius implies the essential conflict between the Romans and the Volsces. The Lieutenant sees the new leader's power as 'witchcraft', something at once supernatural and diabolic. Ironically, it leads to great public unity: the ordinary Volsce soldiers are at one in their enthusiasm for their new hero. None the less, the inevitable effect of this is to cast a shadow over Tullus Aufidius' own reputation.

He realizes that he is, for the moment, the victim of a fall in esteem, but he is helpless so long as he wishes to keep beside him the man without whom his enterprise would fail. The successful conduct of the war is of central importance to him – his own means of defining his personal excellence – and the important implication is that Tullus Aufidius will not let personal and emotional considerations get in the way of its success. This we may choose to see as a reflection on the far grander and more humane actions of the hero later on in the *catastrophe*; Coriolanus cannot finally treat people in the way Tullus Aufidius does.

Coriolanus's pride is once again the subject. It is greater than Tullus Aufidius had imagined it to be (or so he says) when the hero first came to Antium. Precisely how suspicious he was at that moment, how far a detached and calculating distance influenced the welcoming conduct of the Volsce leader, is perhaps questionable, a matter very much for directorial interpretation. Certainly, Tullus Aufidius' current suggestion that he was wary of his rival even at that moment helps to build up an image of a man who is not so naïve as to be taken in by appearances, and we may well choose to see this as a foretaste of the machiavellian image he is now beginning to create for himself. The Lieutenant, we may think, is meant to be impressed.

The very consistency of Coriolanus's pride is a paradox. The man who has deserted to the enemy is, in some respects, 'no changeling', and this very constancy elicits Tullus Aufidius' respect. We feel that he is labouring to do justice to his rival, to define something that is too complex for ready definition but whose very scale and magnificence mean that hatred must be mixed with admiration. Analysis of the problematic nature of the hero keeps him in the audience's mind even when he is not on the stage. The great difficulty of moral judgement – the problems faced when the limits of descriptive language are reached – is powerfully presented.

The Lieutenant, a man whose concept of professional rivalry is altogether less subtle than Tullus Aufidius, again hints at the damaging effect Coriolanus has had on his master's reputation. Tullus Aufidius' response is dark and sinister. He realizes perfectly well what the man is implying and hints at unknown things that he can use to work Coriolanus's downfall. What these might be is far from clear. Perhaps, once again, the mention of them is Tullus Aufidius' attempt to portray himself as a deep and secret schemer, a man whose intentions lie hidden.

Tullus Aufidius himself is obliged to admit that, for the Volsces at least, Coriolanus's actions have indeed been exemplary. His fighting, for instance, has been 'dragon-like'. But for the audience this image of

65

ferocity is compounded with that of the isolation, exile and essential unnaturalness that enveloped it when Coriolanus first applied it to himself, in Act IV scene i. The image harbours a dual implication. The complex nature of the hero is once again evident.

So too is his status as a man of action. We have repeatedly seen the extreme discomfort that language causes the hero, particularly a language concerned with describing and thus in some senses limiting his erstwhile actions. In his wars against the Romans, however, he is action personified. He 'does achieve as soon/As draw his sword'. There is no Hamlet-like uncertainty here. There is no divide between language and action, no hesitation or delay, for there *is* no language. The great soldier as the war-machine is action incarnate. Such a man, we may feel, will inevitably come to grief when trapped in a world that is governed by 'bolted language'.

'Sir, I beseech you, think you he'll carry Rome?' Tullus Aufidius' response to this is one of the richest speeches in the play. He at once acknowledges Coriolanus's martial force, the respect that the patricians have for him and his likely influence on the volatile Citizens and Tribunes:

> I think he'll be to Rome
> As is the osprey to the fish, who takes it
> By sovereignty of nature.
>
> (IV.vii.33–5)

Coriolanus is again seen as a force of nature, an imperious power like the great bird before whom fishes were said to present their underbellies so they could be caught more easily. None the less, his very magnificence produces its own defects. Aufidius shares with Sicinius the insight that Coriolanus cannot 'carry his honours even'. He has a fatal lack of balance, of restraint. There is in his temperament a fatal bias towards self-destruction.

Tullus Aufidius tries to explain this, and the density of his language and syntax suggest the difficulties of a man wrestling with a profound and ultimately elusive problem. He lists the possible causes of Coriolanus's weakness: 'pride', 'defect of judgement' and a 'nature' which cannot change from being a soldier to a politician. We might perhaps think of all these as being in some way applicable, yet such is the awe that Tullus Aufidius is constrained to feel in the imagined presence of his great rival that he cannot admit that they are all operative, even though he freely admits that Coriolanus has taints of each. Whatever the origins of the hero's weakness, however, his shortcomings have made him first feared, then hated and finally banished by his city. Even so, his 'merit' is such that it chokes all mention of his faults even as they are being discussed. The equipoise of good and bad renders final judgement impossible. Language has strained at the limits of definition and finally been defeated.

In the world of action, however – the world of politics – men cannot stand in even-handed puzzlement before a hero whose essential qualities evade their full definition. If a man seems sometimes great and sometimes wicked, those who cannot afford the philosopher's distanced objectivity must make of things what they can. Rather than refining words of definition, they must exploit those aspects that are most immediately useful to them; in other words, the pursuit of objectivity is replaced by the pursuit of advantage. Time shows now one side of a man's character, now another. The politician must exploit whatever serves his purpose best.

Besides, as the extremely dense imagery of lines 51–3 seems to suggest, the public recognition of great deeds through language – the praise offered from the orator's throne – seems to consign such actions to history even while praising them. Words kill deeds, and entomb them. Everything (even the great qualities of a hero and the words that praise him) tends to self-destruction:

> One fire drives out one fire; one nail one nail;
> Rights by rights fuller, strengths by strengths do fail.
>
> (IV.vii.54–5)

It is just this inherent tendency to self-destruction that Tullus Aufidius will now attempt to exploit in order to gain advantage over his rival. Having strained at the edges of language and then retreated, we are now in a world of hand-me-down maxims and cynical opportunism where might is right and words and actions must be used to serve what ends they may.

Act V scene i

Now even Rome seems to have abandoned hope in the efficacy of language and action. It appears that neither can reach the heart. Cominius has been sent on an embassy to appeal to Coriolanus for mercy and has failed. Menenius at first refuses a similar task, believing he too will fail. In his all but hopeless despair he turns to the Tribunes and bitterly suggests that they should approach the man they have exiled and kneel before him in the hope of awakening his pity. The idea of action as eloquence is thus established, but in a way that merely suggests its futility.

'He would not seem to know me.' Cominius' words suggest the blank horror of a world without speech and kinship, a world where even names are no longer of account. His subsequent speech develops this idea in a way at once appalling and firmly connected to some of the play's principal themes:

> Yet one time he did call me by my name.
> I urged our old acquaintance and the drops
> That we have bled together. 'Coriolanus'
> He would not answer to; forbade all names;
> He was a kind of nothing, titleless,
> Till he had forged a name i'th'fire
> Of burning Rome.
>
> (V.i.9–15)

Names – those most intimate connections between friends – hover over silence and lose their erstwhile significance. The Roman hero has contrived this to be a meeting between men whose old bonds of unity he denies. He has all but refused to recognize the identity that each used to have. Each is thus a man without qualities. The hero himself, unwilling to use the ambiguous name conferred on him by his homeland, is 'a kind of nothing, titleless'. Stripped of his old identity, he has vowed most horribly to forge a new one in the burning wreck of the city that has denied him.

Appeals to the 'royal' nature of the man also prove fruitless. How can he be expected to use words of pardon towards a state which has banished him as Rome has done? The sheer illogicality of the situation means that language can have no real meaning. The bonds of nature and kinship have been broken. Erstwhile friends such as Cominius are merely 'noisome musty chaff', worthless things to be burned. As Menenius' impassioned outburst suggests, Coriolanus's language denies humanity to those who once surrounded him.

Sicinius, the sometime skilled manipulator of words, begs Menenius not to direct his fury against him, urging him instead to use language in a more positive way:

> But sure, if you
> Would be your country's pleader, your good tongue,
> More than the instant army we can make,
> Might stop our countryman.
>
> (V.i.36–9)

It is profoundly and bitterly ironic to hear this former manipulator of words beg his erstwhile enemy to use language for an honest and patriotic purpose in the hope that it might genuinely move the heart of the man he has the gall to call 'our countryman'. Menenius at first refuses, but Sicinius begs him once again and is seconded by Brutus. The Tribunes, it seems, have suddenly discovered the emotional appeal of patriotism and the possibilities of words sincerely felt.

Menenius fears, however, that he too might return 'unheard'; silence might condemn him too to ineffectiveness and grief. Sicinius replies that at least his effort will earn him good words, the thanks of Rome. Such an appeal to *pietas*, *romanitas* and public fame still has its attraction for an aristocrat. Menenius is now persuaded to take on the embassy and invents the pathetic hope that Coriolanus might be more amenable after a good meal. Once again the belly serves him as an image.

Brutus wishes him well, but Cominius is the wiser man: 'He'll never hear him.' Desperation knows the horrors of silence, a merciless world where language is refused. Cominius' depiction of how the hero, placed on an alien golden throne and stripped of all his identifying Roman qualities, 'faintly' bade him rise and then waved him away with his 'speechless hand', is the very image of humanity denied and language all but silenced. Only the mention of the embassy of the Roman matrons relieves the sense of utter futility and despair.

Act V scene ii

Menenius' embassy to Coriolanus in the enemy camp is overcast by Cominius' assurance that the Roman hero will not listen to the old man. The scene is a bitter revelation of language rendered virtually powerless.

The peremptory order of the guards – the language of command – immediately appears to defeat the old man's longing to 'speak with Coriolanus'. He is told that Coriolanus will 'hear' nothing from Rome and that he will 'burn' the city before he will talk with its inhabitants. Out of the hero's terrible silence issues the threat of a yet more terrible destructiveness.

Menenius hopes that Coriolanus's 'talk' of Rome might have made mention of his own 'name'. Once again an almost talismanic faith is placed in names as an intimate aspect of identity. But Menenius' name is a talisman without power. The guards will not yield.

Menenius then tries to change the guards' minds through reference to another use of language. He declares that he has been the 'book' of Coriolanus's 'good acts'. He likens himself to a chronicle in which heroic greatness is enshrined in words. By suggesting that his 'praise' has been lavished on their general with great generosity, he is trying to suggest the deep regard in which he holds the man. The First Watch, however, replies with a stinging rejoinder that is deeply rooted in the themes of the play:

Faith, sir, if you had told as many lies in his behalf as you have uttered words in your own, you should not pass here . . .   (V.ii.24–6)

Over-generous histories are mere fabrications, a superabundance of untruthful words as powerless in themselves as Menenius' attempts to reach Coriolanus. A barrier of absolute silence – a silence which, it is suggested, is at least free from dishonest reports – lies between the old man and the young hero. Truth lies in might, in the order the Watch have been given not to admit any more Roman embassies. Such silence is cruel and yet, as the First Watch makes clear, it has its own logic:

Can you, when you have pushed out your gates the very defender of them, and in a violent popular ignorance given your enemy your shield, think to front his revenges with the easy groans of old women, the virginal palms of your daughters, or with the palsied intercession of such a decayed dotant as you seem to be?   (V.ii.38–43)

Coriolanus, the Watch declares, 'has sworn you out of reprieve and pardon'. One of the great powers of language is its ability to deny its use to others. In using language in this way Coriolanus is behaving in an entirely comprehensible way, and, indeed, the logic of the situation is really that the Romans' inability to plead for their lives has been wished on them by themselves.

In revealing the powerlessness of Menenius' language, all that this exchange has really done is to make noise – but that in itself is sufficient to catch Coriolanus's attention. He turns to Menenius and questions him curtly, thereby giving the old man the opportunity to deliver his request, to speak.

His speech is short and moving. Opening with a rhetorical flourish, it eloquently and emotionally contrasts the fire with which Coriolanus will burn Rome to the tears that Menenius is shedding while he pleads for the city. He tells how he has been persuaded only with difficulty to make this speech and then relies on his own credit with the hero to have its effect.

The result is the bitterest disappointment. Coriolanus brushes him aside with a single word. Then, in response to Menenius' pained amazement, the hero offers an image of himself which is of the greatest interest. He uses the power of words to deny his connection with natural and human contacts. He believes that through language – through his mere say-so – he can deny all the bonds that have made him a man and re-create himself in a new image. He is now the self-made hero whose loyalties belong to his old enemies. Language has denied nature, a theme which will be of the utmost importance during the climactic meeting with his mother.

Yet the very uttering of this speech denies, in part, its explicit meaning. Though Coriolanus's new identity has been forged in his terrible silence, the presence of Menenius obliges him to talk and, near the conclusion of his speech, he offers the old man a letter. Though the letter only contains terms for the surrender of Rome which are known to be unacceptable – its words, in short, are worthless – the gesture is a recognition of the pull of emotional bonds, the suppressed love the hero still feels. After this very subtle revelation, however, Coriolanus again imposes an absolute and peremptory silence: 'Another word, Menenius,/I will not hear thee speak.'

Coriolanus departs, pointing out to Aufidius how constant his resolve is. Menenius is left in despair. Words have failed, and out of silence will issue the terrifying and seemingly inevitable destruction of Rome. Coriolanus's awesome consistency of purpose is reinforced, once again, by the comments of the Watch.

Act V scene iii

The scene of Menenius' embassy to Coriolanus is of extreme importance in suggesting a number of themes that will be brought to a climax in what is now to follow: the stupendous confrontation between Coriolanus and his mother.

The scene has shown us a hero who tries to deny his 'enemies' the use of language and so forbid them any possibility of human contact. Nature is contradicted by such silence, the silence in which Coriolanus attempts to forge for himself the beginnings of a new personality and a new fame as the great general of his erstwhile foes. Fundamental truths have thus been discounted.

This has been achieved by a two-fold means. On the one hand Coriolanus forbids the use of language to others while, on the other, he uses words to create for himself an unnatural image of consistent inhumanity. Through a sheer effort of will, the hero is living a lie in a world that he has created through his distortion of mankind's most fundamental quality – his ability to use language. Out of this terrible and unnatural distortion of words are likely to issue deeds of the most appalling savagery. Coriolanus is preparing to utterly annihilate the city and the people among whom the true roots of his identity lie.

Such distortions of language and action involve the hero in hideous processes of destruction and self-destruction. None the less we can detect irresolution beneath his appearance of iron determination, and it is precisely this that gives the lie to his resolve and prepares us for the confrontation with his mother. He *is* moved by the presence of Menenius. He *does* give him the letter (albeit its contents are worthless) in recognition of their former love. Humanity stirs in the hero despite himself, and it is just this stirring of all that makes Coriolanus human that will soon be the means of his tragic destruction.

For the moment, however, his dialogue with Tullus Aufidius emphasizes an unnatural loyalty to the Volscian lords. The rival who, we know, is seeking his death, praises his consistency:

> Only their ends
> You have respected; stopped your ears against
> The general suit of Rome; never admitted
> A private whisper – no, not with such friends
> That thought them sure of you.
>
> (V.iii.4–8)

But even here Shakespeare is careful to qualify this hideous suppression of nature and so point to the fundamental irony of the situation. Confident of his resolve, the hero declares:

> This last old man,
> Whom with a cracked heart I have sent to Rome,
> Loved me above the measure of a father,
> Nay, godded me indeed. Their latest refuge
> Was to send him; for whose old love I have –
> Though I showed sourly to him – once more offered
> The first conditions, which they did refuse
> And cannot now accept, to grace him only
> That thought he could do more. A very little
> I have yielded to. Fresh embassies and suits,
> Nor from the state nor private friends, hereafter
> Will I lend ear to.
>
> (V.iii.8–19)

The failure of language and the resolution of the hero are both reinforced

as, denying the small impulses of humanity that have stirred in him, he
gives his word that he will from now on shroud himself in an absolute
refusal of language, a silence and inhumanity from which will proceed
his terrible revenge.

But Coriolanus is forced to break his vow – his word – even in the
act of swearing it. As the women of his family and his young son enter,
their silent eloquence reminds the hero he is a man:

> My wife comes foremost, then the honoured mould
> Wherein this trunk was framed, and in her hand
> The grandchild to her blood.
>
> (V.iii.22–4)

The awakening of natural feeling forces Coriolanus into an anguished
soliloquy in which words of command attempt to control instinct. He is
using language in the effort to force himself into an unnatural role. 'All
bond and privilege of nature, break!' The blithe resolution of his speech
to Tullus Aufidius crumbles in the face of truth.

As he comments on the arrival of his mother, wife and son, the
theatrical status of the action – the sense almost of a play within a play
– becomes evident, along with Coriolanus's own desperation. His attempts to force himself into his unnatural role inevitably end with the
denial of all humanity, truth and logic:

> Let the Volsces
> Plough Rome and harrow Italy! I'll never
> Be such a gosling as to obey instinct, but stand
> As if a man were author of himself
> And knew no other kin.
>
> (V.iii.33–7)

Such solecism is a refusal of nature. It is the assumption of a false role,
and, as Virgilia greets him, the 'dull actor' is unable to summon up the
false lines his invented character requires. The man who prided himself
on his absolute integrity struggles to maintain a part that gives the lie
to his whole being. His difficulties in themselves reveal the unnaturalness
of his deceit, and from now on Coriolanus's words will increasingly
separate themselves from truth and sense until, eventually, he passes
into a defensive and vicious silence. From this, only the voice of natural
feeling will finally rouse him.

This sense of the cleavage between feeling, action and language is
subtly suggested in Coriolanus's words to Virgilia. Love bids him rise,
embrace her and speak to her. Such love is wholly genuine and cannot,

if rightly understood, lead him to destroy her and the city of which she is a part. Coriolanus then proceeds, however, to another non-sequitur. He asks Virgilia to forgive his 'tyranny' – his cruelty, violence and, by implication, his unnaturalness. But how can she do this without also urging him to be merciful on the Romans, the one use of language he absolutely denies her?

Then Coriolanus sees his mother. Even in the midst of this most unnatural episode the voice of nature prompts him to filial respect. He kneels, and Volumnia bids him rise. Gesture, the action of the orator, is of extreme importance to this great rhetorical scene, a point immediately established by Volumnia herself. Having bid her son rise, she then kneels. It is an action of extraordinary submissive eloquence but one which, by its very unnaturalness, its inverting of the true order of nature, points to the unnaturalness of all that is taking place. For a mother to kneel to her son upsets the proper order of the world, and Volumnia's words make this clear even as she acts:

> I kneel before thee, and unproperly
> Show duty as mistaken all this while
> Between the child and parent.
> (V.iii.54–6)

Coriolanus himself, the author of all that is unnatural here, realizes how his mother's behaviour inverts the order of nature and hastens to bid her rise. As she does so, she introduces the others who have come to beg for peace: Valeria and the hero's own son. The situation is such that the contrast between the man and the boy, the father and son, the innocent and the guilty is one of profound pathos. Coriolanus himself ironically underlines this when (like a true father) he expresses the hope that the boy will always behave in an honourable manner:

> The god of soldiers,
> With the consent of supreme Jove, inform
> Thy thoughts with nobleness, that thou mayst prove
> To shame unvulnerable, and stick i'th'wars
> Like a great sea-mark, standing every flaw
> And saving those that eye thee!
> (V.iii.70–75)

Coriolanus wishes his own flesh and blood to fulfil the ideal that he has himself betrayed. Every gesture and speech in the scene underlines the unnaturalness of the hero's behaviour with supremely elegant dramatic economy. Coriolanus, however, has created a situation in which language must be both twisted and denied:

> I beseech you, peace!
> Or, if you'd ask, remember this before:
> The thing I have forsworn to grant may never
> Be held by you denials. Do not bid me
> Dismiss my soldiers, or capitulate
> Again with Rome's mechanics. Tell me not
> Wherein I seem unnatural. Desire not
> T'allay my rages and revenges with
> Your colder reasons.

(V.iii.78–86)

First he forbids his mother to talk and then, tempering so peremptory a command, is obliged to create a highly convoluted sentence which attempts to convey the idea that the fact that he will not agree to save Rome – to do that which he has sworn he will not do – must not be taken by the women as a denial of their request. In his attempt to treat the matrons with some degree of courteous humanity, Coriolanus is trying to make them believe that their requests have not been denied, but that he cannot break the promise he has made before. He must, above all, keep his word.

Such labyrinthine evasion comes very close to being meaningless, and the speech ends with a far blunter assertion: quite simply, the women must neither affront his honour nor tell him how 'unnatural' his behaviour is. In other words, they must keep silent. Volumnia refuses to be smothered in silence, however. She will talk, for even if her request is offered to no effect, the inevitable result will be words of blame levelled by others at the hero's cruel behaviour. Coriolanus partially submits. Aware of both the political and personal import of the speech he is about to hear, he demands that it be made in the presence of Tullus Aufidius. His rival's involvement in the scene is thus carefully reinforced.

Volumnia's mighty speeches are heavily indebted to their source in Plutarch. They are also woven into the play's main themes with great skill. Here, in a work so profoundly concerned with language – language as persuasion, language as action, language as rhetoric – we have a splendid display of oratory. The effect in the theatre is stupendous. There is, first of all, the gravity of the tone and content. To this is added (and added with ever-increasing pathos) the profoundly moving use of simple gestures: kneeling, rising, and the extending of hands. Above all, the sheer length of Volumnia's speeches provides an awe-inspiring sense of the power of language itself, the weight and magnificence – the humanity – of the act of speaking. In a play full of violent action and deceit, the grave stillness and the eventually irresistible force of emotional truth are overwhelming. Here is language used at the height of its power, as a plea to humanity. The tragic irony lies in the fact that its success triggers the climax. In finding that he is a man, Coriolanus works his own destruction.

Volumnia's great appeal begins with a most moving play on the nature of language. Even if she and her attendants were to be silent, she says, their humiliated state would speak eloquently of their plight. Then, with immense dignity, she elaborates on the bitter irony and the personal torment that arise from a mother having to come and beg her son, the man who should be a joy to her sight, to desist from the most unnatural form of conduct.

Such behaviour forces her into a position where the most sacred of all forms of language – prayers and a mother's expression of her love for her son – are alike denied. To speak or pray for her son's success would be to wish ruin on her country; to desire his defeat would be hideously unnatural. Volumnia is thus deprived of some of the deepest resources of language, while her imagination leads her to envisage other appalling contradictions: a defeated son led in humiliation through the city of his birth, or a successful son riding in triumph through the defeat he has inflicted on Rome. Persuasion is all that is left her. And if persuasion fail she must die.

> If I cannot persuade thee
> Rather to show a noble grace to both parts
> Than seek the end of one, thou shalt no sooner
> March to assault thy country than to tread –
> Trust to't, thou shalt not – on thy mother's womb
> That brought thee to this world.
>
> (V.iii.120–25)

Virgilia, that supremely silent figure of moral integrity seconds Volumnia's words, but it is the terrible pathos of the little boy's speech that forces Coriolanus to rise with the intention of going.

But the power of his mother's language makes him stay. Her words have control over his actions. She has revealed the full import of his enormity to him. Now, ever the skilled politician, she reveals her plan: a negotiated settlement for which each side will utter words of gratitude and praise. A united civic language will once again be possible.

> ... our suit
> Is that you reconcile them, while the Volsces
> May say 'This mercy we have showed', the Romans
> 'This we received', and each in either side
> Give the all-hail to thee and cry 'Be blest
> For making up this peace!'
>
> (V.iii.135–40)

Volumnia's words almost certainly fall into silence. For the moment, Coriolanus cannot countenance such a plan, though soon its implementation will prove the cause of his death. Volumnia speaks again. This time she returns to the familiar idea of language as the permanent record of an infamous reputation. She speaks the imagined words of history.

Again she is greeted with silence. 'Speak to me, son.' But there is no reply. In performance, these moments of silence are agonizing. The mighty flow of Volumnia's language falls into an abyss of inhumanity. We see power rendered weak, humanity denied and, increasingly, the hero torn by his own wordless savagery. Volumnia tries to suggest that, godlike, Coriolanus is threatening something far more terrible than he really intends. The response is silence once again. Volumnia then taunts him with being dishonourable. Still there is no reply. She turns to her daughter-in-law. But Virgilia is weeping, is unable to speak, and even her tears fall to no effect. 'Speak thou, boy.' But the mute appeal of little Martius elicits no response from his father. Volumnia is left with personal bitterness with which to taunt the hero, and Coriolanus turns away. Then, in a last, desperate attempt, Volumnia bids the women kneel. It is a gesture designed to shame the hero, a tableau of utter humiliation but one contrived to no purpose:

> This is the last. So, we will home to Rome,
> And die among our neighbours. Nay, behold's!
> This boy, that cannot tell what he would have
> But kneels and holds up hands for fellowship,
> Does reason our petition with more strength
> Than thou has to deny't. Come, let us go.
>
> (V.iii.172–7)

Words and gestures have had no effect. There remains, it seems, only death.

There follows one of the most dramatic and moving stage directions in the whole canon of Shakespeare's work. Coriolanus goes to his mother and 'holds her by the hand, silent'. Nothing could be more

eloquent or more deeply moving. Not words but silence and the most
tender action (an action which at once expresses humanity and the
relation of a son to his mother) reveal the triumph of natural feeling.
Again, in the theatre, the effect is one of almost unbearable pathos.
The action of the hand is the most expressive communication imagin-
able. Coriolanus, the untutored and often uncouth man of action, the
hero self-exiled from his community, rejoins humanity with a gesture
whose power lies in its gentleness. The voice of nature has
triumphed.

Politically, however, the recognition of humanity is a disaster:

> O my mother, mother! O!
> You have won a happy victory to Rome.
> But for your son – believe it, O believe it –
> Most dangerously you have with him prevailed,
> If not most mortal to him.
>
> (V.iii.186–90)

In reverting to his true nature, Coriolanus must be false to the enemies
with whom he treacherously allied himself. He turns to Tullus Aufidius,
tells him he will 'frame convenient peace', and then asks him how a
man could fail to be influenced by such a speech as his mother has
made. Tullus Aufidius' terse reply – 'I was moved withal' – are the first
words he has spoken for a long time. The cynical tone that they can be
given can sound like a denial of the power of language to reach the
heart and rouse humanity.

Out of this willed and brutal indifference, Tullus Aufidius will now
work his rival's downfall. Coriolanus informs him that the peace he has
in mind must be negotiated with his help. Tullus Aufidius' aside,
however, is an expression of a purely machiavellian pursuit of power.
He will ensure that the hero's new-found humanity is the means of his
destruction:

> I am glad that thou hast set thy mercy and thy honour
> At difference in thee. Out of that I'll work
> Myself a former fortune.
>
> (V.iii.201–3)

Act V scenes iv and v

The previous scene ended with Coriolanus's praise of the Roman
matrons. Now, with that mastery of contrast that is one of the distinc-
tive features of the play's construction, we return with Menenius to

Rome and hear his pessimistic report on his failure. Once again Coriolanus is described in terms of death, near-divinity and ruthless action unmediated by words or thought:

> When he walks, he moves like an engine, and the ground shrinks before his treading. He is able to pierce a corslet with his eye, talks like a knell, and his hum is a battery. He sits in his state as a thing made for Alexander. What he bids be done is finished with his bidding. He wants nothing of a god but eternity and a heaven to throne in. (V.iv.18–24)

Sicinius laments that he appears utterly deprived of mercy, and the panic and despair induced by what we now know to be a false image reaches its climax as a Messenger arrives on stage and bids the Tribune fly to his home; the people have already seized Brutus and are subjecting him to the horrors of the mob. Civil unrest is at its height.

The news brought by the Second Messenger, however, immediately reverses the situation. Triumphant music and shouts of victory greet the returning matrons. The patrician party has won a great victory for Rome through the paradox of defeating its own hero. Just as Act II scene i showed the city rejoicing in Coriolanus's victory, so now Rome rejoices in his defeat by his mother. Even Sicinius can join in the general celebration, and the short fifth scene portrays the triumphant return of the ladies themselves.

Act V scene vi

The climax of the play returns us to Corioles. This seems to have been a second thought on Shakespeare's part since references in lines 50, 73 and 80 suggest that the scene was originally laid in Antium, as it is in Plutarch. It is fascinating to see Shakespeare at work in this way and prompts us to ask why the change was made.

The principal reason, of course, is that the symmetry greatly increases the tragic irony. Indeed, the careful attention to symmetry in this last scene – the masterly reuse and development of the play's basic motifs – is a triumph of stagecraft. The fundamentals of the play do indeed constitute its climax; it grows with an inexorable inner and organic logic, while the dramatic effect is deeply satisfying in its economy and balance.

Corioles, of course, was the city where, alone in his awesome martial splendour, the hero won the great victory that placed him at the height of his fortunes. Corioles established his identity as the principal hero of the Romans and gave him his new name. Now, alone in the city once more, Coriolanus is to be robbed first of his name and then of his life. The man of heroic deeds is to be trapped in a web of words and shameful actions. He is to be stripped of his identity and murdered. The contrast with his greatest moment is complete.

The invidious manipulation of language is made clear from the start. Tullus Aufidius instructs his attendants to go to 'the lords o'th'city' and present them with a paper in which he has explained the charges he is levelling at his great rival. These, it later emerges, suggest that Coriolanus has, in his own person and believing this to be invested with the authority of the Volscian rulers, negotiated a dishonourable treaty with the Romans without consulting the Volsces themselves. However, if this is indeed the substance of Tullus Aufidius' charges then it is in flat contradiction to Coriolanus's own careful assertion at the close of Act V scene iii that he would be advised in the matter of negotiations by Tullus Aufidius himself. Indeed, he had asked him to 'stand to me in this cause'. It is possible, of course, that Coriolanus's own supremicist nature, the subject of much of the dialogue here, actually led to his arrogant handling of the talks, but such details are not germane to Shakespeare's purpose.

The dramatic effect he is seeking is the suggestion of ruthless dishonesty and betrayal. Tullus Aufidius is to appear shamefully manipulative. A disadvantageous peace has been concluded with the Romans, and Tullus Aufidius is determined to use it as the means of working the hero's destruction. The machiavellian opportunism he swore to follow at the end of Act IV scene vii is now becoming apparent.

The cynicism of this is underlined by Tullus Aufidius' readiness to go to the market-place where he will 'vouch the truth' of his accusations to both the Lords and the Volsce citizens. The contrast to Coriolanus's reluctance to go to the Roman market-place and win the 'voices' of the people is the measure of the two men. Tullus Aufidius, we feel, can perform in the market-place with all the manipulative cynicism of a Roman Tribune. He knows, too, that he must get there before his rival who also 'Intends t'appear before the people, hoping/To purge himself with words'.

It is in the market-place, of course, and again shouting out his familiar language of self-aggrandizement and scorn, that Coriolanus will die. Once again the symmetry enhances the effect of tragic inevitability, and Shakespeare furthers this in the dialogue that takes place between Tullus Aufidius and the conspirators. As so often in the play, this section develops several major themes simultaneously.

There is, first of all, the rivalry between the two men, the clash of

personalities that mirrors the broader political situation. Tullus
Aufidius' role as a manipulator of words is also developed. He presents Coriolanus's supremacy over him as the actions of a man profoundly ungrateful to one who has offered him 'charity'. While this is
not absolutely untrue, the effect it has (and which Tullus Aufidius intends it should have) is to portray himself as a man hard-done-by. In fact,
the situation is rather more complex than this. Coriolanus's greatness is
a force in nature and not the product of calculation. Besides, Tullus
Aufidius originally offered him 'charity' in order to secure a great ally
in the war with Rome. He was hardly the disinterested man of mercy.

Now we learn that he is plotting Coriolanus's shameful death.
Again the symmetry underlines the tragic irony. The first encounter
between the two men that the play presented was their fight at the
close of the battle scenes, in Act I scene viii. Here, despite his use of
'condemnèd seconds', Tullus Aufidius had failed to defeat his rival.
Now, at the close of the play, he will employ a similar ruse and kill
him.

Once again, 'the people' become a subject of conversation. Tullus
Aufidius, suddenly turned populist in his cynical pursuit of his own
advantage, mentions that he cannot proceed against Coriolanus without
knowing their opinion: 'We must proceed as we do find the people.'
There is an element of common sense in this – the people do indeed
regard the Roman as their hero – but the volatility of their opinions
makes their views of little worth. As the Third Conspirator makes clear,
they will follow where right is might. One of the play's fundamental
themes is thus reiterated.

Tullus Aufidius then tries to offer a portrait of Coriolanus as a
smooth and duplicitous flatterer:

> I raised him, and I pawned
> Mine honour for his truth; who being so heightened,
> He watered his new plants with dews of flattery,
> Seducing so my friends. And to this end
> He bowed his nature, never known before
> But to be rough, unswayable and free.
>
> (V.vi.21–6)

This is patently absurd. There is absolutely no warrant for these
accusations, and the Third Conspirator, moved to correct so blatant a
falsehood, begins to mention Coriolanus's 'stoutness' when he stood
for consul. With the quickness of a born deceiver, a cunning manipulator of words, Tullus Aufidius immediately develops this subject. 'That

I would have spoke of.' He very deftly gets his lies back on the right
track and paints once again a vivid picture of how his own reputation
has been diminished by Coriolanus's presence.

Though a machiavellian to the core, Tullus Aufidius skilfully exploits
the vocabulary of a culture of honour and shame to present himself as
an aggrieved aristocrat. We are now prepared for his most deplorable
ruse – his interpretation of the titanic scene between Coriolanus and his
mother:

> At a few drops of women's rheum, which are
> As cheap as lies, he sold the blood and labour
> Of our great action.
>
> (V.vi.46–8)

This is a downright and cruel lie. Magisterial language and profound
pathos and nobility – words and deeds that reawakened a love of peace
and humanity – are seen here as a little matter of dishonest snivelling.
Language could hardly be more cynically abused. One of the great
moments in the play is remembered in this, the last scene, only to
degrade it.

The return of Coriolanus to the city is heralded by drums, trumpets
and great shouts. Again the mastery of stagecraft is remarkable. We
have not seen the hero for many lines and, on the last occasion, he was
the obedient, loyal and loving figure who had rediscovered humanity in
the presence of his mother. Now, having negotiated a peace between
the two opposing political forces, he enters once again in seeming
triumph. He utters measured words of peace and reconciliation in the
market-place:

> Hail, Lords! I am returned your soldier,
> No more infected with my country's love
> Than when I parted hence, but still subsisting
> Under your great command. You are to know
> That prosperously I have attempted and
> With bloody passage led your wars even to
> The gates of Rome. Our spoils we have brought home
> Doth more than counterpoise a full third part
> The charges of the action. We have made peace
> With no less honour to the Antiates
> Than shame to th'Romans. And we here deliver,
> Subscribed by th'consuls and patricians,
> Together with the seal o'th'Senate, what
> We have compounded on.
>
> (V.vi.71–84)

But the document is immediately discarded by Tullus Aufidius, its words set at naught. The language of diplomacy is denied:

AUFIDIUS   Read it not, noble Lords;
              But tell the traitor in the highest degree
              He hath abused your powers.
CORIOLANUS Traitor? How now?
AUFIDIUS   Ay, traitor, Martius!
CORIOLANUS   Martius?
                                        (V.vi.84–7)

Just as in the moments preceding his banishment Coriolanus was condemned as 'a traitor to the people' and was stung by the name into the full violence of his fury, so here the use of the same word rouses him to the same reaction. But there is a further taunt: he also loses the name which enshrined his ambiguous identity as a hero. Once he is no longer Coriolanus, his true awesomeness as a 'son of Mars' asserts itself. As Tullus Aufidius accuses him of treason, of breaking his word, of being irresolute in his nature and pathetically under the influence of his mother, the hero calls on his god: 'Hear'st thou, Mars?' But even this association is denied him: 'Name not the god, thou boy of tears!' The hero is no more than a 'boy', someone weak and insignificant, rightly under the control of his mother. He is neither god nor monster nor man. It is this threat to his manhood, to his identity, that rouses the hero to his final self-destructive act of fury. Though at first he tries to restrain himself (an act pathetically ironic in the context of the play as a whole) the essential nature of the hero bursts forth with a terrible violence:

              Cut me to pieces, Volsces. Men and lads,
              Stain all your edges on me. 'Boy'! False hound!
              If you have writ your annals true, 'tis there
              That, like an eagle in a dove-cote, I
              Fluttered your Volscians in Corioles.
              Alone I did it. 'Boy'!
                                        (V.vi.112–17)

Here so many of the hero's quintessential qualities are exposed: the self-destructive yet magnificent fury of pride and honour slighted by shame, the essential isolation, the aggressive and bestial solecism, the hatred of lies, the concern with honest history, language as violent action. It is an outburst at once pathetic and awe-inspiring, flawed and glorious, heroically self-assertive and disastrously self-destructive. The titan in the

83

market-place is for one final time the victim of the manipulated voices of the people. Their erstwhile hero is once again the lone man they want to destroy.

A Second Lord begs for peace and asks the screaming mob to consider the hero's nobility and fame. He craves a 'judicious hearing' for the offences that may have been committed. He beseeches Tullus Aufidius to 'trouble not the peace'. But these words of moderation have to be shouted above a crowd for whom language is now an expression of violence. The hero himself draws his 'lawful sword' and, in the very moment of initiating violent action, is struck down. He is ignobly slaughtered by a crowd of conspirators in the city he had heroically captured. As the Conspirators scream 'Kill, kill, kill, kill, kill him!', language, action, violence and deceit are one, and then, in the most degrading action of all, 'Aufidius stands on him'.

We feel both horror and pity at this ignoble tableau: horror at the deceit and wanton destructiveness, pity that a man so awesome yet so faulted should have been slaughtered in this way. The words of the two Volscian Lords express something of our emotions, but it is Tullus Aufidius who finally rises above them for the tragedy's concluding words. 'My noble masters, hear me speak.' Claiming to be blinded by his rage, he informs the Volsces that they will soon learn the great danger that the hero posed to the state. Meanwhile, he will go obediently to the Senate and either excuse himself or be condemned. Tullus Aufidius portrays himself as the most loyal of state servants, the man whose language is justly tailored to the time. As the Volscian Lords bear away the hero's corpse, the dead march and the trailing pikes create a sombre funeral pomp suited to a hero. Tullus Aufidius is left to speak the play's closing words:

> My rage is gone,
> And I am struck with sorrow. Take him up.
> Help three o'th'chiefest soldiers; I'll be one.
> Beat thou the drum, that it speak mournfully.
> Trail your steel pikes. Though in this city he
> Hath widowed and unchilded many a one,
> Which to this hour bewail the injury,
> Yet he shall have a noble memory.
> Assist.
>
> (V.vi.148–56)

Death and fame are woven together in a noble epitaph for a hero, but even as these words are spoken we may wonder if this manipulator of words and deeds is fitting his language to the time and acting as appearances dictate he should. Such are the ambiguities of language and action in Shakespeare's unillusioned view of the ultimately tragic world of politics.

Coriolanus and Seventeenth-century Politics

It now remains to be seen how far this highly political drama reflects the political events of the period in which it was written. To do this effectively, we need to create for ourselves an image of England that is very different to our present one, a country which had much in common with the modern Third World. We must think of an under-developed and agrarian economy where labour was cheap, ineffi-ciently exploited and dependent on the seasons. We must think of a soci-ety where production and technology were at low levels, where capital was relatively scarce and, far from being channelled into profitable enterprises, was often lavished on conspicuous consumption – a consump-tion designed to emphasize social rank and flamboyant distinctions of class. This was a world where paternalistic ideas of hierarchy and rigid notions of obedience were made visible by a hundred gestures of deference, where those who lived 'idly . . . without manual labour and . . . bear the port, charge and countenance of a gentleman' were con-sidered qualitatively different to their workers, who, like children, they could beat for disobedience.

But we need also to consider a country in which, against these rigid notions, profound social changes were occurring and divisions opening up which would lead eventually to civil war. We need to think of a country with a rising population to feed and a hugely expanding capital city, a country in which an articulate middle class was becoming ever more influential, and in which the aristocracy, while clinging to vast resources of ancient power, were none the less facing a crisis of identity. In other words we need to think of an England that bears striking analogies to the tense and troubled Rome of *Coriolanus*.

As far as England was concerned, the death of Elizabeth I (some four or five years before the original production of the play) had made obvious what was already becoming clear during the previous two decades: the social and religious settlement to which Elizabeth gave her name had been precariously maintained by her political skill alone. It had settled affairs only by leaving too many issues undiscussed, and it was increasingly inadequate for a period of fast and profound social change.

While Elizabeth herself had skilfully played her royal sceptre against the parliamentary mace, trodden an ambiguous and even cynical path between the perils of religious extremism, and held foreign powers at bay by a combination of indomitable bravery and wily vacillation, the succession of James I signalled the shift towards a politics of more open confrontation. It was not until the late 1620s that this became a marked prelude to the Civil War and the eventual trial and execution of Charles I in the name of 'the people of England' on the treasonable charge of violating 'the fundamental constitution of the kingdom'. However, a number of general characteristics and some particular events in the early years of James's reign have a bearing both on this change of political temper and the responses that might have been roused by *Coriolanus* among the heterodox and highly articulate audience that crammed the Globe.

We will deal with the general considerations first. A continuing and dramatic rise in the population, the need to feed these people, and a change in the patterns of property ownership whereby more and more land was 'enclosed' and came under the exploitation of private enterprise, resulted in the creation of a large class of landless day labourers. While such people were perhaps slightly better treated than their continental counterparts – particularly during periods of unemployment which were, none the less, appallingly savage – the poor were almost powerless in a situation of rising prices and falling wages. They were, in the words of Professor Stone, 'in the state of abject misery which found intermittent relief in rioting and mob violence'. One such riot, occurring contemporaneously with the likely date of Shakespeare's work on *Coriolanus*, was the so-called 'Midlands Insurrection' of 1607, a small and pathetic attempt by landless labourers to counter enclosure, and a move possibly provoked by a corn shortage. Corn prices were certainly high in the west during this period, and by the middle of the following year there was a similar problem in Warwickshire.

With the latter came renewed anti-enclosure threats. Writing to the Earl of Salisbury at this time, a correspondent mentions 'the dearth of corn, the prices rising to some height, caused partly by some that are well stored'. These complaints, the letter-writer continues, make the people 'arrogantly and seditiously' to speak of the oppressive conditions of their lives, just as the 'mutinous Citizens' do in Act I. The implicit attitudes to the labouring classes revealed here – the belief in their lowly station in a sanctioned hierarchy, the concern with order and the horrors of protest – are of the greatest significance to our understanding of *Coriolanus*, and a relation between the opening of the play and such events as are described by the Earl's correspondent is very probable.

The likelihood of such a relation is strengthened by the fact that, for these opening scenes, Shakespeare altered his source, playing down Plutarch's picture of a people troubled by usury and, instead, emphasizing and wholly reinterpreting their complaint as a powerful and even dignified protest against a shortage of corn. There were purely artistic reasons for Shakespeare's alterations to his sources, but, to an audience aware of the Jacobean social climate, Shakespeare's particular handling of this episode must have had great topical relevance. Indeed, the strong hostilities that these scenes have aroused down the ages are an important witness to the power of the play, and there is every reason to suppose that their effect on the original audience must have been equally disturbing.

A second aspect of the rise in population and the expansion of the economic sphere which bears on *Coriolanus* is the growth in the size of London, a growth unparalleled by the capitals of other European countries. Economically, politically and in terms of professional resources, London dominated the kingdom. This huge development, bringing with it a rise in the pressures of urban living and the problems of social control, was bound to focus interest on that great classical paradigm of the city: Rome, whose tumultuous history was the common knowledge of an increasingly educated and literate nation, and whose political vocabulary entered the language of contemporary debate. The idea of Rome as being at once a mighty historical force, a centre of values and a pulsating human environment viciously divided against itself will again be of great significance to the play.

Two further results of the expansion of the population and the economy that have a bearing on *Coriolanus* are increased social mobility both up and down the scale at this period and, in particular, the rise of the mercantile, professional and gentry classes with their resulting insistence on having a voice in the running of the country through Parliament. The relation of power to new 'voices' swelling the ranks of the Senate and of such voices to the manipulatable, ephemeral and stinking breath of the plebeians, is an important aspect of the imagery of *Coriolanus*. It suggests some guiding attitudes to contemporary events that we shall have to examine.

The newly augmented wealth and articulacy of the gentry is the most important single political force in the period, and, in its turn, it caused a radical reappraisal of such men's relation both to the aristocracy and to the Crown. We are clearly dealing here with a period of deep social change, and we should look first at how these matters affected the titular aristocracy – Menenius' 'we of the right-hand file'. In so doing, we may gain some further notion of how the social and political pressures in the play might have related to those in contemporary England.

The much debated 'crisis of the aristocracy' at this period is reflected in the profound change away from automatic deference towards its members, the numbers of whom were to be increasingly inflated by the creation of new titles. As de Tocqueville remarked of the French Revolution, upward social mobility of this sort creates particularly hostile resentment among the old élite, who consequently assert their traditional power ever more aggressively. However, the old power and influence of the English aristocracy, though it remained considerable, none the less declined as the values of rents from their estates fell and their local importance receded. The nobility further lost much of their military power, through their loss of control of potential soldiers, and often failed to keep abreast of the technical competence to lead a contemporary war. A powerful assertion of the exclusive prowess of the aristocracy is, of course, central to *Coriolanus* and provides further parallels between the play and contemporary social and political conditions.

The aristocracy sold their land in an effort to maintain their extravagant lifestyle, a lifestyle designed to assert their status in a world where this was being questioned. Here we might think of Menenius' self-portrait as a 'humorous patrician' known for his lavish feasts with his peers. The aristocracy attempted to recoup such expenditure through the harsh financial practices of enclosure and the purchase of monopolies (the right to the sole production of staple goods), which in turn threatened the loyalty and affection of their poorer tenants particularly. The words of the First Citizen about the creation and distribution of wealth in Roman society are most instructive here:

Care for us? True indeed! They ne'er cared for us yet. Suffer us to famish, and their storehouses crammed with grain; make edicts for usury, to support usurers; repeal daily any wholesome act established against the rich, and provide more piercing statutes daily to chain up and restrain the poor. (I.i.77–82)

Such a confrontation between a class of threatened 'haves', deeply concerned with their status and power, and an equally aggressive and troubled class of 'have nots' is central to the world of the play and is also reflected in the world of its first audience.

In addition to the features already mentioned, Professor Stone writes of the nobility: 'Other causes of the decline in respect for the aristocracy were the undermining of their electoral influence because of the rise of deeply felt political and religious issues; their increasing preference for extravagant living in the city instead of hospitable living in the country-side; and growing doubts about their attitudes, real or apparent, to-wards constitutional theory, the methods and scale of taxation, forms of worship, aesthetic tastes, financial probity and sexual morality.' This is an impressive onslaught, a picture of a class losing its special aura, growing out of touch with new sources of power and, by its behaviour, threatening the validity of the accepted forms of social cohesion. While the insights of a modern historian are unlikely to match exactly the concerns of a Jacobean playwright, there is none the less much in Professor Stone's analysis that corresponds to the issues concerning the aristocracy in *Coriolanus*.

There is, in *Coriolanus*, a defiant emphasis on the status, mystique and military prowess of the threatened aristocracy; the belief, hurled in the faces of questioning Tribunes and an unsettled populace alike, that it is the aristocracy alone – an élite group seemingly personified by Coriolanus himself – who are truly Roman and who embody the fundamental, quasi-spiritual values of *romanitas* which entitle them to rule. These beliefs form the substance of Cominius' eulogy to the hero on the battlefield, with its emphasis on those central ideals of deeds and fame which are treasured by noble people and are reluctantly accepted by the Tribunes and the populace as the acme of the race:

> If I should tell thee o'er this thy day's work,
> Thou't not believe thy deeds. But I'll report it
> Where senators shall mingle tears with smiles;
> Where great patricians shall attend and shrug,
> I'th'end admire; where ladies shall be frighted
> And, gladly quaked, hear more: where the dull tribunes,
> That with the fusty plebeians hate thine honours,
> Shall say against their hearts 'We thank the gods
> Our Rome hath such a soldier.'

(I.ix.1–9)

This speech is an excellent example of a ruling class reinforcing its particular values by praising an individual who is, by their standards, exemplary. It is of particular relevance to the Jacobean social context since it is a defiant celebration of the idea that the special mystique of the aristocracy is proved on the battlefield. In the England in which *Coriolanus* was first produced, as we have seen, this idea was under attack and was, indeed, a central crisis for the aristocracy, some of whom were seeking a new justification for their privileged existence, one which would replace the old and now outdated chivalric ideal of the noble warrior hero. Cominius' speech is thus the assertion of a way of life that the nobility could no longer take for granted.

To appreciate how this notion of an élite and aristocratic martial group appeared to a contemporary audience we need first to question our modern idea that a person's worth is often valued largely by financial status and the place that he or she occupies in the hierarchy of production. We need, rather, to appreciate a quite different system of relationships, one based on received ideas of order and degree in which status, as Robert Mousnier has expressed that matter in *Social Hierarchies*, is defined 'not according to the wealth of . . . members . . . nor yet by their role in the process of production of material goods, but according to the esteem, honour and rank that society attributes to social functions that can have no connection at all with the production of material goods'.

Esteem, honour and rank as the causes and rewards of military heroism are precisely the basis of the aristocratic mystique admired by Cominius. He sees them apparently embodied in Coriolanus, and this emphasis accounts for the horror which this representative aristocratic hero feels when he is obliged to descend to the market-place, the locality of trade, in order to have his worth assessed by labourers. This crucial moment in the play can thus be seen as the juxtaposition of two irreconcilable views. On the one hand there is the popular voice that has been manipulated into questioning the hero's apparent worth, and on the other Coriolanus's own downright assertion of the aristocratic mystique and its belief in its own self-evident and non-negotiable military values that justify its claim to power. Coriolanus in the market-place shows these values at their extreme. In so doing, he also reveals the terrible social and political risks that attend so absolute and divisive a gesture.

How familiar would a contemporary audience have been with this sort of display? Knowledge of the personalities of the time makes it clear that such a domineering figure would not have been unknown. The proud and martial aristocrat, early trained to the wars, whose assertion of those very values that made him so magnificent also made him hated and feared, was indeed a recognized phenomenon. There is, for example, the glittering figure of the Earl of Essex (beheaded 1601), while the sentimental portrait of Sir Walter Ralegh (beheaded 1618) as the aristocrat who threw his cloak in the mud for his queen is far from the only view of him held by his contemporaries. While his bravery was recognized (in a way that is irresistibly reminiscent of Coriolanus, he joined the French wars at the tender age of fourteen), Ralegh was, as

John Aubrey declared, 'damnably proud'. At the turn of the century, ballads circulating in London accused him of extortion and contempt for the poor, while as early as 1586 a figure calling himself 'A.B.' described the way in which Ralegh handled his monopoly of cloth and Cornish tin production. A.B. depicts Ralegh's place among his labourers, 'a rough and mutinous . . . multitude, 10,000 or 12,000, the most strong men of England'. The proper governor of such a throng, A.B. says, should be one 'well accounted of, using some familiarity, and abiding amongst them'. But it was not so, apparently, with Ralegh:

. . . no man is more hated than him; none cursed more daily by the poor, of whom infinite numbers are brought to extreme poverty through the gift of cloth to him. His pride is intolerable, without regard to any, as the world knows; as for his dwelling amongst them, he neither does nor means it, having no place of abode.

A.B. saw very clearly the danger in a position where a great soldier is also a great anti-populist: 'In time of service, this head must either fight without a body, or else the members will cut off such a head.'

We are very close here both to the 'mutinous members' described by Menenius and to the image of Shakespeare's hero. It is thus possible and indeed proper to see *Coriolanus* partly – but only partly – in terms of the social and political crisis that threatened the aristocracy's power and influence in early seventeenth-century England.

But to this picture of a dangerously proud, exploitative and insecure nobility on the one side and a working class desperately poor and rebellious on the other, we need to add a third element: the rise of Parliamentary influence during the reign of James I especially and, with this, the declining influence of the aristocracy in the face of the gentry's concern with political, religious and constitutional issues. We need, in other words, to see if there is any relation between the early seventeenth-century Parliament at Westminster and Shakespeare's presentation of Sicinius and Brutus, the Tribunes of the people. We shall discover that such an analogy does indeed exist and that the language of politics in the play is often the language of politics in the period when it was written.

The latter point is illustrated by King James himself who, opening the second session of the Commons in 1605, described certain truculent Members as 'Tribunes of the people, whose mouths could not be stopped'. Since the proceedings of Parliament were naturally followed with avid interest (despite the difficulties of obtaining precise information) it is reasonable to suppose that the contemporary significance of the phrase 'Tribunes of the people' would have been appreciated by a quick-witted London theatre audience. Further, since the monarch uttered the phrase during an important constitutional crisis, it is appropriate to examine the background to see what context this might offer for the play.

The reign of James I saw the start of the true rise of Parliament as a self-conscious political force reacting against the corruption of the 'Court' party and, by asserting its powers to consent to taxation and vote on new legislation, forming an opposition that was eventually to be established as the 'Country' party. In a period when corruption in the bureaucracy was threatening respect for the traditional institutions of government – bribery was, for example, endemic at all levels – the presence of Parliament as the unrivalled, elected and representative body of public opinion was bound to enhance its prestige. It grew in size, was attended with alacrity and, by being summoned with increasing frequency, developed both new confidence and a series of procedural techniques which gradually freed it further from the influence of the Crown.

The Commons increasingly demanded the right to initiate discussion and influence policy. They were aided in this by the lawyers who packed its benches and sought in ancient statutes for the precedents that allowed them to express innovatory demands and win the initiative in decision-making. Based on medieval concepts of protecting the liberties of private interests against the state, the antiquarian researches of such men as Sir Edward Coke developed the idea of a 'balanced' constitution, an effective Parliament to set against the prerogative rights of the Crown.

In this respect it is interesting to consider the reverence with which the Tribunes in *Coriolanus* apparently respect the ancient tradition of showing wounds in the market-place while using this as a smokescreen for their own political concerns. As such, it is possible to compare them to those who, in the Jacobean Parliaments, were now establishing careers for themselves as leaders of the Commons' business. Although it was only in the 1620s that such conflicts became an open and divisive hostility between the Crown and Parliament, the issue was declaring itself at the session in which James uttered his remarks about 'Tribunes of the people'.

One further factor needs to be added to this discussion of the rise of Parliamentary influence, and that is the nature of its alliance with Puritanism.

The relative laxity of many of the Elizabethan clergy had created a vacuum of religious zeal which had been partly filled by Puritan ministers who emphasized independence of judgement based on private conscience and Bible reading. Such attitudes had an obvious effect on an interest in the morality and conduct of public institutions, and were adopted by some nobles, gentry and greater merchants. They were also popular among the lower classes, people who again responded to a call for 'a holy violence in the performing of all duties'. With the consequent gradual transfer of allegiance away from the roundly asserted divinity of the king towards a concept of 'godly' magistrates sitting in the House of Commons, confidence could develop in the righteousness of the Puritan cause and efforts to question the established order.

While most of the leading Puritans believed strongly in the traditional hierarchies of society and very few indeed wanted the sort of participatory democracy apparently urged by the Tribunes, Puritan insistence on popular literacy and preaching helped to encourage the politicizing of urban artisans. The result was a deep hatred of this growing force among conservatives and a belief, as a contemporary anti-Puritan expressed it, that 'Puritanism is the root of all rebellions and disobedience, untractableness in parliament etc., and of all schism and sauciness in the country.'

This is a somewhat extreme statement, and to appreciate it fully we need to consider the ways in which the social and political forces we have been discussing were received by people of the early seventeenth century. We must examine, in other words, the climate of opinion which, while it may seem to have overstated trends as they really existed, none the less became, by its influence, a historical fact. Imagined terrors, after all, can be just as influential as threats that actually exist.

The fear of a rebellion inspired by Puritanism was widespread in early seventeenth-century England and, associated with the 'levelling' ideals of the continental Anabaptists especially, quickly became branded as an enemy force within society. Homilies 'Declared and Read, by all Parsons, Vicars, and Curates, Every Sunday and Holy Day in Their Churches' emphasized the sinfulness of rebellion and provided a propagandist interpretation which firmly suggested that God never allowed revolutions to prosper.

The ease with which it was believed that dissatisfaction could be aroused is shown by the great Elizabethan churchman Hooker, who declared: 'He that goeth about to persuade a multitude that they are not so well governed as they ought to be, shall never want attentive and favourable hearers.' Such popular rebelliousness was also shown by Shakespeare in *Henry IV, Part One* as being the product of

> ... poor discontents,
> Which gape and rub the elbow at the news
> Of hurlyburly innovation.
>
> (V.i.76–8)

In this, Shakespeare's attitude is wholly conventional. The belief that London in particular was a fruitful seed-bed of such dangerous activity is suggested by a proclamation issued following the revolt led by the Earl of Essex:

... there is at this time disbursed within our city of London and the suburbs thereof a great multitude of base and loose people, such as neither have any certain place of abode, nor any good and lawful cause of business to attend hereabouts, but lie privily in corners and bad houses listening after news and stirs and spreading rumours and tales, being of likelihood ready to lay hold of any occasion to enter into any tumult or disorder, thereby to seek rapine and pillage.

It is against this background – tense, highly emotional in tone and yet far from wholly realistic in content – that we should begin to examine the possible relationship between an extreme conservative view of the rise of Puritan influence in Parliament and the democratic efforts of the Tribunes in *Coriolanus*. We can do so best by returning to the proceedings of Parliament in 1604–5 when James spoke out against the 'Tribunes of the people, whose mouths could not be stopped ... from the matter of the Puritans'.

What had caused the dissension in Parliament was the issue of the 'purveyance': the supply of goods and income to the royal household at rates assessed by the Royal Purveyors. This had long been a source of discontent and, as a problem which centred around the antagonism between the Crown's prerogative powers to raise its resources through Parliament and of MPs to finally approve these levies, was necessarily a cause of friction. Matters came to a head in 1604 when Parliament set up a committee to draft a bill restraining the Royal Purveyors. The bill was duly prepared by John Hare and Lawrence Hyde and presented to the King, who rejected it as an encroachment on the royal prerogative.

Members of Parliament responded with a remarkable document: the *Apology of the House of Commons, made to the King, touching their Privileges*. This contains much strongly worded protest, but, more importantly both for future developments and for the relation of

Coriolanus to contemporary events, it also expressed a new formulation of an old idea: the notion that the voice of the people is the voice of God, *vox populi, vox dei*. This important doctrine had previously been taken to mean, in the words of Hooker, that

> the general and perpetual voice of man is the sentence of God himself. For that which all men have at all times learned, Nature herself must needs have taught; and God being the author of Nature, her voice is but his instrument.

However, by the turn of the century the phrase had undergone a significant modification. It was now the voice of the people as it was expressed through Parliament that was believed to be the voice of God. Parliament, being the representative institution of the people (at least of the relatively few entitled by age, gender and property qualification to vote), was their voice. We should compare such a revolutionary step to the speech uttered by Sicinius at the moment of his greatest power and folly, when he exiles Coriolanus:

> in the name o'th'people
> And in the power of us the Tribunes, we,
> Even from this instant, banish him our city,
> In peril of precipitation
> From off the rock Tarpeian, never more
> To enter our Rome gates. I'th'people's name,
> I say it shall be so.

> (III.iii.99–105)

To a contemporary audience, the parliamentary language here would have been particularly redolent, while the speech itself, of course, is a searing criticism of the man who utters it. The popular voice he claims to represent has been manipulated by a self-seeking politician who, though he indeed speaks for the people, has fashioned their 'voices' to be the means of his own advancement. The *vox populi*, far from being the voice of God, is merely the squawk of an irresponsible demagogue.

As on stage, so – in the view of some at least – in Parliament. As an early seventeenth-century correspondent wrote of the Commons' activities over the purveyance: 'If your lordship had heard them, you would have said that Hare and Hyde had represented the tribunes of the people.' A great political debate had thus been joined in terms that exactly reflect those of *Coriolanus*, and fundamental questions of sovereignty – the problem of whether power centred around the Crown or Parliament – had been expressed in the vocabulary of ancient Rome.

But we can go yet further with our comparison. In his crucial speech in Act III scene i, Coriolanus himself, clearly seeing the appointment of the Tribunes to the Senate as a threat to aristocratic sovereignty, speaks also for a seventeenth-century Court party similarly threatened by the rise of the Commons:

> I say again,
> In soothing them we nourish 'gainst our Senate
> The cockle of rebellion, insolence, sedition,
> Which we ourselves have ploughed for, sowed, and scattered
> By mingling them with us, the honoured number,
> Who lack not virtue, no, nor power, but that
> Which they have given to beggars.
>
> (III.i.68–74)

The speech, the intricate thought and subtlety of which denies the common assumption that Coriolanus himself is merely a proud and inarticulate soldier, follows exactly the conservative Elizabethan view of the question of sovereignty taken by such men as Sir Thomas Elyot. In the *Boke called the Governur* Elyot again discussed this issue in terms of ancient Rome:

> ... the communality more and more encroached a licence, and at the last compelled the Senate to suffer them to choose yearly among them governors of their own estate and condition, whom they called Tribunes; and under whom they received such audacity and power that they finally obtained the highest authority in the public weal, in so much that often times they did repeal the acts of the Senate ... Finally, until Octavius Augustus had destroyed Antony, and also Brutus, and finished all the Civil Wars ... the city of Rome was never long quiet from factions or seditions among the people ... If the nobles of Rome had not been men of excellent learning, wisdom, and prowess, and that the Senate, the most noble council in all the world ... had not continued and with great difficulty retained their authority, I suppose verily that the city of Rome had been utterly desolate after the expelling of Tarquin.

Peace can only be guaranteed, it is suggested here, through the power of one sovereign ruler. By the time of the first production of *Coriolanus*, some important elements in public opinion were beginning to change their views on this issue and move tentatively towards the idea of a limited participatory democracy which, it was hoped, would avoid the excesses of aristocratic absolutism on the one hand and the instability of easily-manipulated mass opinion on the other. This was the crisis that would eventually lead to the English Civil War in the middle of the seventeenth century. *Coriolanus* is a very early intimation of these profound historic changes.

Bibliography

Two excellent and readily available editions of *Coriolanus* are those edited by G. R. Hibbard (The New Penguin Shakespeare, 1967) and Philip Brockbank (The Arden Shakespeare, 1976). All references in this book are to the former edition.

For the background to rhetorical humanism see J. B. Trapp, 'Education in the Renaissance' and 'Rhetoric in the Renaissance' in A. G. Dickens et al., *Background to the English Renaissance* (Gray-Mills Publishing, London, 1974); Isabel Rivers, *Classical and Christian Ideas in English Renaissance Poetry* (Allen and Unwin, London, 1979); and Peter Burke (ed.), *The Renaissance Sense of the Past* (Edward Arnold, London, 1969). For Rhetoric, see especially Peter Dixon, *Rhetoric*, The Critical Idiom Series No. 19 (Methuen, London, 1971). An interesting attempt to relate rhetoric to acting may be found in Bertram Joseph, *Elizabethan Acting* (Oxford University Press, Oxford, 1951).

For the background to Shakespeare's Roman plays see Robert S. Miola, *Shakespeare's Rome* (Cambridge University Press, Cambridge, 1983). An excellent introduction to the tragedies generally is G. K. Hunter, 'Shakespeare and the traditions of tragedy' in Stanley Wells (ed.), *The Cambridge Companion to Shakespeare Studies* (Cambridge University Press, Cambridge, 1986). This volume also contains the excellent 'Shakespeare and the arts of language' by Inga-Stina Ewbank.

Interesting and important discussions of the play include D. J. Gordon, 'Name and Fame: Shakespeare's Coriolanus' in G. I. Duthie (ed.), *Papers, Mainly Shakespearian* (Oliver and Boyd, London, 1964); Brian Vickers, *Shakespeare: Coriolanus* (Edward Arnold, London, 1976); and Adrian Poole, *Coriolanus*, Harvester New Critical Introductions to Shakespeare (Harvester-Wheatsheaf, New York, 1987).

Studies of the contemporary political background include W. Gordon Zeeveld, '*Coriolanus* and Jacobean Politics', *Modern Language Review* 57 (1962). Jonathan Dollimore, *Radical Tragedy: Religion, Ideology and Power in the Drama of Shakespeare and His Contemporaries* (Harvester Press, Brighton, 1982), provides some challenging insights. Lawrence Stone, *The Causes of the English Revolution: 1529–1642* (Routledge and Kegan Paul, London, 1972) provides essential material.

FOR THE BEST IN PAPERBACKS, LOOK FOR THE 🐧

In every corner of the world, on every subject under the sun, Penguin represents quality and variety – the very best in publishing today.

For complete information about books available from Penguin – including Puffins, Penguin Classics and Arkana – and how to order them, write to us at the appropriate address below. Please note that for copyright reasons the selection of books varies from country to country.

In the United Kingdom: Please write to *Dept E.P., Penguin Books Ltd, Harmondsworth, Middlesex, UB7 0DA.*

If you have any difficulty in obtaining a title, please send your order with the correct money, plus ten per cent for postage and packaging, to *PO Box No 11, West Drayton, Middlesex*

In the United States: Please write to *Dept BA, Penguin, 299 Murray Hill Parkway, East Rutherford, New Jersey 07073*

In Canada: Please write to *Penguin Books Canada Ltd, 2801 John Street, Markham, Ontario L3R 1B4*

In Australia: Please write to the *Marketing Department, Penguin Books Australia Ltd, P.O. Box 257, Ringwood, Victoria 3134*

In New Zealand: Please write to the *Marketing Department, Penguin Books (NZ) Ltd, Private Bag, Takapuna, Auckland 9*

In India: Please write to *Penguin Overseas Ltd, 706 Eros Apartments, 56 Nehru Place, New Delhi, 110019*

In the Netherlands: Please write to *Penguin Books Netherlands B.V., Postbus 195, NL–1380AD Weesp*

In West Germany: Please write to *Penguin Books Ltd, Friedrichstrasse 10–12, D–6000 Frankfurt/Main 1*

In Spain: Please write to *Alhambra Longman S.A., Fernandez de la Hoz 9, E–28010 Madrid*

In Italy: Please write to *Penguin Italia s.r.l., Via Como 4, I-20096 Pioltello (Milano)*

In France: Please write to *Penguin Books Ltd, 39 Rue de Montmorency, F-75003 Paris*

In Japan: Please write to *Longman Penguin Japan Co Ltd, Yamaguchi Building, 2–12–9 Kanda Jimbocho, Chiyoda-Ku, Tokyo 101*

FOR THE BEST IN PAPERBACKS, LOOK FOR THE 🐧

PENGUIN POETRY LIBRARY

Arnold   Selected by Kenneth Allott
Blake   Selected by W. H. Stevenson
Browning   Selected by Daniel Karlin
Burns   Selected by Angus Calder and William Donnelly
Byron   Selected by A. S. B. Glover
Clare   Selected by Geoffrey Summerfield
Coleridge   Selected by Kathleen Raine
Donne   Selected by John Hayward
Dryden   Selected by Douglas Grant
Hardy   Selected by David Wright
Herbert   Selected by W. H. Auden
Keats   Selected by John Barnard
Kipling   Selected by James Cochrane
Lawrence   Selected by Keith Sagar
Milton   Selected by Laurence D. Lerner
Pope   Selected by Douglas Grant
Rubáiyát of Omar Khayyám   Translated by Edward FitzGerald
Shelley   Selected by Isabel Quigley
Tennyson   Selected by W. E. Williams
Wordsworth   Selected by W. E. Williams

FOR THE BEST IN PAPERBACKS, LOOK FOR THE 🐧

PLAYS IN PENGUIN

Edward Albee	**Who's Afraid of Virginia Woolf?**
Alan Ayckbourn	**The Norman Conquests**
Bertolt Brecht	**Parables for the Theatre (The Good Woman of Setzuan/The Caucasian Chalk Circle)**
Anton Chekhov	**Plays (The Cherry Orchard/Three Sisters/Ivanov/The Seagull/Uncle Vania)**
Henrik Ibsen	**Hedda Gabler/The Pillars of the Community/The Wild Duck**
Eugène Ionesco	**Rhinoceros/The Chairs/The Lesson**
Ben Jonson	**Three Comedies (Volpone/The Alchemist/Bartholomew Fair)**
D. H. Lawrence	**Three Plays (The Collier's Friday Night/The Daughter-in-Law/The Widowing of Mrs Holroyd)**
Arthur Miller	**Death of a Salesman**
John Mortimer	**A Voyage Round My Father/What Shall We Tell Caroline?/The Dock Brief**
J. B. Priestley	**Time and the Conways/I Have Been Here Before/An Inspector Calls/The Linden Tree**
Peter Shaffer	**Lettice and Lovage/Yonadab**
Bernard Shaw	**Plays Pleasant (Arms and the Man/Candida/The Man of Destiny/You Never Can Tell)**
Sophocles	**Three Theban Plays (Oedipus the King/Antigone/Oedipus at Colonus)**
Arnold Wesker	**Plays, Volume 1: The Wesker Trilogy (Chicken Soup with Barley/Roots/I'm Talking about Jerusalem)**
Oscar Wilde	**The Importance of Being Earnest and Other Plays (Lady Windermere's Fan/A Woman of No Importance/An Ideal Husband/Salome)**
Thornton Wilder	**Our Town/The Skin of Our Teeth/The Matchmaker**
Tennessee Williams	**Cat on a Hot Tin Roof/The Milk Train Doesn't Stop Here Anymore/The Night of the Iguana**

FOR THE BEST IN PAPERBACKS, LOOK FOR THE

PENGUIN LITERARY CRITICISM

A Lover's Discourse Roland Barthes

'*A Lover's Discourse* ... may be the most detailed, painstaking anatomy of desire we are ever likely to see or need again ... The book is an ecstatic celebration of love and language and ... readers interested in either or both ... will enjoy savouring its rich and dark delights' – *Washington Post Book World*

The New Pelican Guide to English Literature Boris Ford (ed.)

The indispensable critical guide to English and American literature in nine volumes, erudite yet accessible. From the ages of Chaucer and Shakespeare, via Georgian satirists and Victorian social critics, to the leading writers of the 1980s, all literary life is here.

The Theatre of the Absurd Martin Esslin

This classic study of the dramatists of the Absurd examines the origins, nature and future of a movement whose significance has transcended the bounds of the stage and influenced the whole intellectual climate of our time.

The Theory of the Modern Stage Eric Bentley (ed.)

In this anthology Artaud, Brecht, Stanislavski and other great theatrical theorists reveal the ideas underlying their productions and point to the possibilities of the modern theatre.

Introducing Shakespeare G. B. Harrison

An excellent popular introduction to Shakespeare – the legend, the (tantalizingly ill-recorded) life and the work – in the context of his times: theatrical rivalry, literary piracy, the famous performance of *Richard II* in support of Essex, and the fire which finally destroyed the Globe.

Aspects of the Novel E. M. Forster

'I say that I have never met this kind of perspicacity in literary criticism before. I could quote scores of examples of startling excellence' – Arnold Bennett. Originating in a course of lectures given at Cambridge, *Aspects of the Novel* is full of E. M. Forster's habitual wit, wisdom and freshness of approach.

FOR THE BEST IN PAPERBACKS, LOOK FOR THE 🐧

PENGUIN CRITICAL STUDIES

Described by *The Times Educational Supplement* as 'admirable' and 'superb', Penguin Critical Studies is a specially developed series of critical essays on the major works of literature for use by students in universities, colleges and schools.

titles published or in preparation include:

SHAKESPEARE
Antony and Cleopatra
As You Like It
Hamlet
Julius Caesar
King Lear
Measure for Measure
A Midsummer Night's Dream
Much Ado About Nothing
Othello
Romeo and Juliet
Shakespeare's History Plays
Shakespeare – Text into Performance
The Tempest
Troilus and Cressida
The Winter's Tale

CHAUCER
Chaucer
The Nun's Priest's Tale
The Pardoner's Tale
The Prologue to the Canterbury
  Tales